I0085775

When The Church Stones Its Leaders

Restored From The Wounds Of Ministry

Steve & Michelle Bunkoff

When The Church Stones Its Leaders,
Restored From The Wounds Of Ministry
Copyright 2017 by Steve and Michelle
Bunkoff. All rights reserved. Except for brief
quotations for review purposes, no part of
this book may be reproduced in any form
without prior written permission from the
authors.

Visit wwwstevebunkoff.com to order
additional copies.

New American Standard Bible Scripture
quotations marked (NASB) taken from the
New American Standard Bible®, Copyright
© 1960, 1962, 1963, 1968, 1971, 1972, 1973,
1975, 1977, 1995 by The Lockman
Foundation Used by permission.

(www.Lockman.org)

Dedication

This book is dedicated to our daughters, Denise and Meredith, who suffered with us through this trial more than anyone will ever know. Our love and prayers are with you as you continue to find your way.

We also dedicate this book to the men and women of our church who stood with us in the crucible, never believing the accusations, encouraging us to the end – even to their own hurt. Thank you for your loyalty and love through the darkest period of our lives.

ACKNOWLEDGMENTS

We want to thank Ken Bangs for speaking the prophetic words to our hearts that resurrected the writing of this book and put it on the front burner again. We also appreciate his many words of affirmation and practical steps to complete the job.

Jackie Macgirvin at ChristianBookDoctor.com has been a fantastic editor and encourager to us. We were blown away by her ability to take our rough draft and fine-tune it, turning it into a great finished product. You've been so gracious to answer our questions and walk us through the process of getting our book published. Thanks!

I want to thank Emily Lam for the professional job she did with the layout and artwork for the front and back cover.

Emily Lam, https://emilytlam.com

ENDORSEMENTS

When The Church Stones Its Leaders, hits the bull's eye when it comes to helping wounded church leaders. Steve and Michelle have risen from the ashes of pain and betrayal and desire to come alongside other leaders who are still smoldering. They ask the hard questions: *Where was God during my crisis?* but more importantly, they answer them. They lay out a healthy process to forgive from the heart. They explain eight things that God has done through their lives because of their devastating experience. Michelle also writes matter of factly to overlooked and overworked wives. In a tragedy like this, your choices determine your end result -- better or bitter. Steve and Michell's advice can guide you around the pitfalls that can slow you down or derail you permanently.

Jackie Macgirvin, M.A. Author, The Designer Bag at the Garbage Dump & Angels of Humility

Steve and Michelle are personal, lifelong friends, and it's an honor to endorse their book. Their story is interesting and also forthright—because they have nothing to protect. They've taken the things they've learned in their journey and distilled them into principles for surviving and overcoming disappointment. Not only will you glean from them, but their story will confirm that the path you're on leads to healing and wholeness. Like them, you're going to emerge from your trial a wholehearted lover of Jesus Christ!

Bob Sorge, Author, Bobsorge.com

My wife Cathy and I thank God that Steve and Michelle came to our small town to pastor their first church. Their influence on our spiritual lives has been immeasurable. We still minister to other lives daily, using the tools they taught. It's great to see the wisdom God has poured into them for so many years, finally being put together in this book. As one who was forced to resign from a pastoral position, it's refreshing to finally see someone provide ministry to not only pastors but to their families.

Robert J. Donk, Director of Mentor Services, Marriage Resource Center of Frederick County, MD

"Well done my good and faithful servant". How many of us long to hear those words from the mouth of our Savior, but as pastors, how many of us feel as if we have

fallen short of our calling, or perhaps even abandoned our calling, and are fearful that we will never receive that approval. Perhaps the pain inflicted on us and our families was too much, and so in a move of preservation, we bailed. In crafting "When The Church Stones Its Leaders", Steve and Michelle Bunkoff have been amazingly transparent in the pain, but also the process of healing that they have experienced as pastors. My wife and I have known them almost from the beginning of their ministry, and we have walked together with them through some of the same experiences, they in their church, and we in ours. We are told "God looks at the heart, not the numbers", but the reality is that we can't help measuring our "success" by worldly standards, especially when denominations, or church conferences, or books, or articles, or magazines all promote "how you can do it better". This results in an accumulation of unrealized vision, prophetic promises that seem unfulfilled, and ultimately feelings of bitterness arising from thoughts of a life of sacrifice that didn't seem to yield much fruit.

Steve and Michelle address these thought patterns, incorrect beliefs, and offer an entry point onto the path of healing. Each will move at their own pace, in their own timing, and perhaps even their own measure of success, but this book provides a sharp and to the point assessment of where you are, and then takes you by the hand and walks you through the process of becoming whole again. When you feel like you gave all you could but came up short, take encouragement from this work. Thank you, Steve and Michelle.

Carl and Jeannine Nelson, Pastors Emeritus

Because the church accepts people as they are, faults and all, it is filled with cowards and worse. There are far too many who harm and abuse those for whom Christ died and who have given themselves wholly to His cause. God has never hidden or excused the faults and sins of His followers no matter their level of authority. The prophet Nathan confronted King David because he had orchestrated the death of the faithful warrior Uriah. David found forgiveness for his sin but the irreparable damage was done to his kingdom and his family.

It is not just church members who get wounded; elders, deacons, pastors, and overseers are vulnerable as well. In fact, the greater the investment, the greater the risk and the potential for hurt. Unfortunately, the effects of wounded leaders extend to those they lead. It is especially damaging to the Kingdom when overseers cause hurts or fail to protect those under their charge. That God still claims as His own this spotted institution we know as the Church is a testimony to His grace and longsuffering.

Steve & Michelle Bunkoff are authorities on this topic. Having paid the price of experience and survived, they can speak hope and healing to those who have been wounded by church people. I have had the joy of seeing them conquer many of the snares the enemy laid before them as they pressed forward to experience total healing and restoration.

Their story is not finished; their victory is still unfolding and like Jacob of old, they walk with a limp. But they have chosen to use their limp to help others overcome their own hurts and to point the way to restoration. This is more than the testimony of their journey; they have identified the milestones on the journey to freedom and victory for those who would be whole again.

This book speaks wisdom and warning to church leaders at all levels who have been given the charge of leading and protecting God's children.

When the Church Stones its Leaders is a must read for every church leader.

Larry D Holland Church Consultant and Associate Pastor, Covenant Church, McKinney, TX

FORWARD:

Veterans of the Armed Services all share in the experience of having served, and that is both honorable and commendable. These servants of the Republic have much in common and are able to commiserate one with the other concerning these common experiences. But the veteran who has experienced combat, who suffered the emotional and physical wounding of battle has walked in a place, which cannot be understood by those who have never seen the battle.

We can chat, but you cannot go vicariously into that with which my flesh, my mind, and my spirit are forever filled.

Christians are a lot like veterans. All who have answered the call to follow Christ can share in common experiences gained in obedience to the *Great Commission.* But only those who have surrendered to the call to full-time ministry and have suffered the wounds of the daily battle against every weapon in the enemy's arsenal can fully understand Christ's admonition to the twelve in John 15:20: "'*No servant is greater than his master.' If they*

ix

persecuted me, they will persecute you also...."

Pastors know from experience that the question is not *will* I suffer the wounds of ministry but *when, how often* and *will I survive?*

Steve and Michelle Bunkoff are *veteran pastors* who share with Paul the ability to say, *"Now I rejoice in what was suffered for you, and I fill up my flesh what is still lacking in regard to Christ's afflictions, for the sake of His body, which is the church... of which I became a minister..." (Colossians 1:24 – 25).*

They have suffered wounding from friendly fire and from the forces of powers and principalities. Yet they are not weakened or scared. They are victorious survivors who now offer other pastors the benefit of their combat experience.

As one who has survived combat both in the field and the pulpit, I count it a higher honor and privilege to endorse this work. It is an essential tool in the survival pack of all who choose to become a minister of His body, which is the church.

Kenneth W. Bangs, D. Min.

Table Of Contents

APPENDIX 141

INTRODUCTION

This book is the story of a season of our lives which lasted for nearly ten of the 35 years which Michelle and I shared in pastoral ministry. Had we known back in 1974, when we went to Bible school, what we were going to go through, I'm not sure we would have signed on the dotted line. But like most Christian leaders that we know, we felt called by the Lord to the ministry and believed that we could truly bring hope and change to people and advance God's Kingdom. We went for it wholeheartedly and without reservation. As you can probably guess by the title of this book, it didn't exactly work out like we'd planned. Perhaps only eternity will tell how effective we were.

During those years we served in five churches, two of which we pioneered. In the early days of pioneering, there were times when I preached that there were more people on the worship team staring at my back than in the congregation gazing adoringly at me. Our three children served faithfully with us in those early years. In one church that we pioneered, I played guitar, Michelle played keyboard, our 13-year-old son played drums, and our two girls greeted people and handed out bulletins. We personally set up for the services as a family, led the worship, preached, taught in Sunday school, did the visitation, strategized, administrated, did nearly all the physical work around the church building, gave more financially than any other family and prayed for God to break in on us. It was rough and ugly, but we loved it. Most pioneer pastors can relate.

This book, however, is not about pastoring or church planting. It's not another book giving you 15 principles to grow your ministry or ten ways to resolve church conflict. This book is for wounded leaders who feel like their guts have been wrenched out and they have been left all alone, bleeding. It is written for church leaders who somehow have been caught in the machinery or politics of the church organization and have come out the other side, sometimes still wondering *What happened?* Our goal is to identify with your pain, share some of ours, and offer some practical help for processing your pain on the way to healing.

We have written in a straightforward, honest manner. We are not interested in being politically correct or sounding spiritual. This is a book formed in the midst of a church crisis, actually, several. George Barna and other sources report that there are some 1500 pastors who leave the ministry every month -

- some 18,000 per year. This book is for them and the countless other youth pastors, missionaries, church administrators and worship leaders who have also been through the battle -- and often times, left for dead at the side of the road.

It has been said, "The church is the only army that shoots its wounded." Someone a little more honest -- probably a church leader -- took it a step further saying; "First they wound you -- *then* they shoot you." Of course, we recognize that this not only applies to church leaders but members as well, but this is not that book.

We hope that by writing about our own journey we can bring some insight, some hope, and some encouragement to your wounded heart. Our goal is to help church leaders make sense of what has happened to them. I must admit that during and after our crisis in the mid-90's, the last thing we wanted to do was to hang out with any believers, go to any church meetings, hear any sermons or read any Christian books. We wanted to crawl into a corner and lick our wounds. Perhaps you can relate. It seemed like there was no one to talk to, few resources to help us process our pain or encourage us to know that we would eventually come out the other side. The thought of being somewhat healthy again and back in church seemed next to impossible and honestly, at that point, pretty undesirable.

Understanding the place, you may currently be in, we promise to keep it short and simple.

Also, I want to set the record straight right up front. If you feel that we are writing this book with some sort of vendetta against the church, you have misunderstood our hearts and motives. Although there have been times when we did not like church people very much, we totally believe that God *will* have a pure and spotless Bride. We believe that there is a needed, radical change coming to the Body of Christ and that she will reflect the glory of God and be found acceptable and holy in His sight. We believe the vision expressed by Mike Bickle from the International House of Prayer in Kansas City, that "God will change the understanding and expression of Christianity in one generation." That glorious day is coming, and we can't wait!

We also want to say that the circumstances of our crisis are presented from our perspective, but we related them as accurately as we could. Perhaps the others involved saw things differently. In our opinion, however, they did not have the advantage of knowing the full story because they did not walk with us through it from the beginning or go behind the scenes.

Our prayer is that in reading this book you will find a place to process your wounds and find new hope in God, even if things seem hopeless now.

4

"To dwell above with the saints we love, that will be glory. To dwell below with the saints we know, well that's a different story."
Irish proverb

CHAPTER ONE

Our Story

It was the summer of 1971. Michelle and I had been married two years and things were rocky already. I was only 19, which explains a lot. Michelle was struggling with depression, a condition that predated her meeting me.

Then one day, Michelle had an amazing encounter with God. Reading through Kathrine Kuhlman's book, *I Believe In Miracles*, God's presence came into our living room and dramatically touched her. I was at work, so I knew nothing about the incident. It didn't take long, however, for me to realize that something was different. Michelle was no longer depressed. Not only wasn't she depressed, she had a joy that I'd never seen before. Along with joy, there was also peace, mercy, understanding, and grace! Where had my wife gone? It took only six weeks of this *weird* behavior before I had to ask her, "What's come over you?" A few days later I found myself weeping before the Lord as the cleansing, forgiving power of God washed over my heart.

We became different people. All we could do was read our Bibles and talk about the Lord. God began to heal our marriage and our family. We began attending church, joined home groups and shared with others what happened to us. These were great years, filled with excitement, joy and a growing sense that God had something in store for us.

It wasn't long before we felt the call of God to go into full-time ministry. We were so excited. We even left a decent size family construction business, started by my grandfather, to follow our dreams. Married with three young children, we set off to fulfill His calling at Bible School. God's hand seemed to be upon us and before graduating we received the invitation to pastor our first church.

It was a small country church, within driving distance of the Bible school, incorporated about 75 years earlier, denominational in its roots. It was well established and safe. The townspeople there were simple, country folk. In looking back, I sometimes liken it to riding our first bike -- complete with training wheels. We would have had to do something really crazy to derail that church. Excited to be serving the Lord, we put our hands to the plow, prayed for wisdom and began. The Lord blessed our efforts and in the five years we were there the church tripled in attendance, people met the Savior and as leaders, we were blessed to be a part of that ministry. We still maintain friendships with some of those members.

After about four and a half years we began to feel a stirring in our hearts that a change was coming. I had been attending a local community college with the goal of earning a Bachelor's Degree. We felt that this was the time to resign the church and head to Rochester, NY to complete that goal. After graduating with a BA in Religion and Philosophy and reflecting on our first church experience, Michelle and I realized that what we really wanted was to plant a church that would allow us the freedom to follow the Lord's leading, uninhibited by tradition or constrained by someone else's vision. I spoke with our denomination's US Ministry's Department and was given three potential locations. Of that three only one was not in a rural setting, and being city folk we decided to check out the location with the larger population.

Within a few months of relocating, we took our first steps to establish a church. For the first few months, we met in an aerobics' center with floor to ceiling mirrors. It was a small beginning, but we were excited about the prospects of growing and building the church there. As those of you know who have planted a church, we counted heavily on our family serving with us. It was a great time for us as we saw God's plans coming together. After ten years of pioneering there, God was blessing us and we grew to over 200 in attendance (large for that area of the country) and were averaging about 10 to 15 new visitors each week.

Our hearts were beginning to come alive with fresh expectation. Our ministries included an in-church bookstore, a pre-K nursery school, a food pantry to help the poor, and numerous small groups. Because we had pioneered the ministry from scratch, the church had our DNA and it was a rewarding place for us to be. The atmosphere was charged with God's presence, the congregation was loving, and life was good. We would have been content to remain there the rest of our lives, endeavoring to bring the Kingdom of God to our community, seeing lives impacted and radical disciples established in that area. It was about that time that we hit a brick wall. It seemed like one week everything was going great, and the next week everything was falling apart.

> The atmosphere was charged with God's presence, the congregation was loving, and life was good.

After surviving the devastation of the fire that completely destroyed our next church building we rolled up our sleeves and began to regroup and rebuild. It was during this time that someone in leadership accused us to our area denominational leadership. We were accused of lying, control, larceny, heresy and several counts of sexual misconduct. It was even rumored that I had something to do with the arson fire. If I recall, there were about 30 charges listed on the paper presented to us in a meeting with our area denominational leaders. *We were shocked to say the least!* An investigation began. We were told to remain silent and tell no one about it. After three long months our denomination concluded that there was no proof that any of the accusations were true, but even so, they still ordered us to take a three-month leave of absence; then "we could return to our church pulpit" once again. Although we disagreed with their decision, we wanted to maintain a submitted heart, so we took the leave.

During those three months, our denomination also required that I see a clinical psychologist, as they suspected/insinuated that I had some kind of "disorder." After several sessions and tests, including sessions with Michelle, the psychologist concluded that I was completely normal. What a relief! (Michelle knew better but that stuff doesn't show up on tests!) He told my wife and me that he was convinced that I was the victim of religious and politically motivated individuals who would not rest until they had received a report that whatever disorders I had were now taken care of. Unless they received the report, they wanted, they would just dismiss his findings and proceed until they found a cooperating counselor -- and so, his required report to them said what they wanted to hear.

It wasn't until after all of this that it was reported to us by members of the church council that a plan was in place by some of our denominational overseers intending that we never return to the church. Again, *we were shocked*! Meanwhile, during our absence, continued questions and rumors spread throughout the community and the church. The denomination had appointed an interim pastor, who we later found out was working against us. When a question was raised about us he would only answer "There is much more below the surface than anyone really knows." This effectively undermined our integrity and the unanswered questions allowed people to follow their suspicions and draw their own conclusions.

During that same three-month period, the interim leader did several things in the church that he was not authorized by anyone to do. He saw that the constitution, the leadership team, and the membership role was changed. These changes along with his comments effectively assured our dismissal. By the time our three-month sabbatical was over, instead of just returning to the pulpit as we were promised, we were now required to candidate at our own church -- the very church we had pioneered. And, we needed to get a nearly unanimous vote of approval to return -- another new stipulation put in place by the interim. As part of the candidating process, we sat through a six-and-a-half-hour meeting in which vitriolic questions were hurled at us by members of the congregation that we had loved and sacrificed for. The pain of this unjust and ungodly inquisition again crushed our hearts. Michelle and I left that meeting physically ill.

Although we had remained silent during the sabbatical as directed, once we were past that time, we began to have some of the church members and board members come to us openly questioning the motives of the interim pastor and the ethics of the process. Much of it did seem unethical, as well as a clear violation of the church constitution, and all with the underlying purpose of removing us from ever pastoring there again.

In our desire to remain submitted to our overseers, we requested that the denominational leaders look deeper into what had really gone on in our absence, but it wasn't long before we were asked to leave, and our credentials revoked for daring to raise these concerns. The denominational leadership never did talk to us or the board members in the church who felt the process was wrong. The final straw was that we were forced to withdraw our candidacy from pastoring at the church as the interim pastor had added a clause to the constitution that only those carrying credentials with that denomination could pastor there.

So, we were out of the church, our reputation was destroyed in the town by gossip and rumors, and we were thrown out of our denomination. Perhaps the rejection of our denomination caused the deepest part of our pain. You see, it wasn't just a denominational affiliation for us; this was our spiritual home. We had attended their Bible school in the 70's. We had wholeheartedly supported them over the years. Our deepest friendships had been built among the people there. To us -- they were family.

Looking back, we knew that there would be battles in ministry, but we never expected to be hit from behind by those we loved and trusted. I could so identify with the pain and devastation that William Wallace felt when he was betrayed by Robert the Bruce in *Braveheart*. Needless to say, I was devastated, my wife was devastated, and our daughters, who were then in their early 20's, were also devastated.

CHAPTER TWO

What's Happening in the Western Church?

"Houston, We Have A Problem"

Whether your story is more or less tragic than ours, it's sad to know that our story and your story are not isolated incidents. There are thousands of church leaders who have gone through similar situations. This is the unfortunate testimony of church leader after church leader. And let's not forget, this is more than just another church statistic; this is about people. This is about pastor's wives whose hearts have been shredded to pieces, leaders whose dreams have been crushed, and the children of those leaders who grow up hating the church and sometimes even hating God as a result of what their parents went through. This is about congregations that are torn apart and shame coming to yet another church in the community. A leader we respected said to me, "Oftentimes in attempting to bring correction, denominations and church leaders focus on the issues and forget that there is a family

14

involved." These families are being impacted in profoundly detrimental ways.

> **"No one who is not in the ministry knows the price you have paid as a pastor."**

If these were isolated incidents, we might chalk it up to personality differences. Perhaps someone went into the ministry for the wrong reasons. Some leaders may even be charlatans or somehow deserve what happened. But the truth is that most leaders who have been wounded in ministry are wonderful men and women who have sensed a genuine call of God. They may not be perfect, but they have served sacrificially, with integrity, love, and compassion. They sacrifice their time, their finances, their comfort and sometimes even their families for the sake of the church that Jesus loves.

One pastor friend of mine said to me during our crisis, "No one who is not in the ministry knows the price you have paid as a pastor." And when there are so many pastors sharing very similar stories, we cannot help but come to the conclusion that there is something wrong in the western church. Too many sincere men and women of God have gotten chewed up and spit out by the machinery of the church or the denomination. Too many have been wounded by those who have said "Pastor, we're behind you!" Years ago, our friend Bob Mumford told me, "You never know whether those behind you are following you or chasing you." Although humorous at the time, in the end, it turned out that they were chasing, and they weren't happy.

What is happening in the American church?

In his book *Clergy Killers,* G. Lloyd Rediger says, "One informed estimate is that a pastor is forced out of the ministry every six minutes in the United States."

Here are some of the statistics that we've gathered from church organizations posting on the internet and in church leadership publications. We especially appreciate Barna Research Group for their outstanding work with clergy in the western church, across denominational lines, in this regard. Here are some of their findings:

Barna Research Group reports that 1500 pastors leave the ministry *every month*. They don't change churches, they leave the ministry. That's over 50 per day or roughly 18,000 annually. Some might say that clergy have the highest casualty rate of any profession. The research distilled from Barna Group, Focus on the Family and Fuller Seminary, showed the following results:

1500 pastors leave the ministry each month due to moral failure, spiritual burnout, or contention in their churches.

97% of pastors have been betrayed, falsely accused or hurt by their trusted friends.

94% of pastor's families feel the pressure of the ministry.

50% of pastors' marriages will end in divorce.

80% of pastors feel unqualified and discouraged in their role as pastor.

50% of pastors are so discouraged that they would leave the ministry if they could but have no other way of making a living.

80% of seminary and Bible school graduates who enter the ministry will leave the ministry within the first five years. Only 10% will actually retire from a ministry vocation.

70% of pastors constantly fight depression.

70% said the only time they spend studying the Word is when they are preparing their sermons.

90% of pastors report working 55 - 75 hours per week, often getting a sub-standard salary.

<u>OTHER CONFIRMING CHURCH LEADERSHIP STATS:</u>

ON LONELINESS:

More than 70% of pastors do not have a close friend with whom they can openly share their struggles.

ON BURNOUT:

The dominant cause for pastors to leave the pastoral ministry is burnout. Number two is moral failure.

William Moore in a study of 341 clergy from 36 denominations and 43 states showed that unrealistic expectations are a major factor in pastor burnout.

ON EDUCATION AND TRAINING:

Only 50% of pastors felt that the education they received adequately prepared them for ministry. Most pastors rely on books and conferences as their primary source of continuing education.

90% felt inadequately trained to cope with ministry demands.

ON FAMILY:

94% felt under pressure to have the "ideal" family 80% of pastors believe the pastoral ministry has negatively affected their families

Marriage Problems Pastors Face:

81% insufficient time together
71% use of money
70% income level
64% communication difficulties
63% congregational differences
57% differences over leisure activities
53% difficulties in raising children
46% sexual problems
41% Pastor's anger toward a spouse
35% differences over ministry career
25% differences over spouse's career
ON STRESS AND EMOTIONAL PRESSURE:

25% of all pastors don't know where to go for help if they have a personal or family conflict or concern.

Here's an excerpt from the August 1998 issue of James Dobson's newsletter:

Our surveys indicated that 80% of pastors and 84% of their spouses are discouraged or are dealing with depression. More than 40% of pastors and 47% of their spouses report that they are suffering from burnout, frantic schedules, and unrealistic expectation.

75% reported a significant stress-related crisis at least once in their ministry and 40% reported serious conflict with a parishioner at least once a month.

One year the Southern Baptist paid out $64 million in stress-related claims, second in dollar amounts only to maternity benefits.

ON CHURCH DROPOUT:

1500 leave the ministry every month

In 1998, James Dobson Ministries reported "an estimated 1500 pastors leave the ministry every month.

At any given time, 75% of pastors in America want to quit.

In response, we cannot just look at the numbers and shake our heads in disbelief. And again, each statistic represents men and women who have been rejected, wounded, or set aside in shame. It represents people who can find no one to turn to or confide in for fear of rejection. Too often behind the statistics, there are children who have been crushed right along with their parents, many of them never able to be restored to the church or to the Lord. And in addition, behind each of these stories are church members who have also been deeply wounded. After twenty-five case studies where a small group of antagonists succeeded in forcing the Senior Pastor to be dismissed, Dennis Maynard said, "After removing a senior pastor from the church, the result is that there is a loss of nearly one-half of the active members. He goes on to say that "Most congregations spend decades trying to recover from the divisions caused by antagonists."

Sadly, these struggles happen privately. Why such secrecy when it comes to the pressures and problems of spiritual leadership? Have we built a system with such high moral, ethical, and religious standards that even the Apostle Paul would struggle to attain it? Pastors are put on pedestals and the religious zealots have no tolerance for mistakes or human weakness. Of course, it's all done in the name of holiness, which is impossible to argue against. Should there be a standard that we follow? Of course; but let me gently remind you how many men and women God chose and used -- from Genesis through Revelation -- who didn't have it all together and who struggled with human weakness. In fact, God seems to like working with imperfect leaders.

> ## Conflicts in the church may be normal. but incivility and abuse are not.

So, when leaders find themselves facing personal struggles, why don't they share their pain or seek help? Perhaps embarrassment or the fear of gossip leads some to avoid seeking counseling. The fear of rejection and concerns about loss of membership, respect or honor may discourage transparency. And of course, sometimes leaders just don't open up because of pride.

This Is A Growing Phenomenon

We hate to admit it but conflict in the church is normal. Conflicts have been in the church since the church was birthed in the first century. I think it started about the time the first human being joined up. You've probably jokingly said, there is no perfect church and if you find one please don't join it because that will be the end of it.

I recently read that even Jonathan Edwards, one of the most brilliant men in Colonial America, who the Lord used as one of the leading voices in what was later called the Great Awakening, was voted out of his church! He was actually considered America's first and possibly one of the greatest theologians of his day. Thousands were converted to Christ during his ministry, but someone in his congregation spearheaded the termination of the man that God was using to bring revival to an entire nation.

I agree with G. Rediger who said; "Conflicts in the church may be normal. But incivility and abuse are not".

GOING INTO MORE DETAIL

A Nationwide Study

A nationwide study among Protestant pastors publish by the Barna Research Group in the July 10, 2006, issue of *Research Releases in Leaders & Pastors* indicated seven intriguing insights about how pastors think of themselves and the churches they lead. We will look at the top six findings. These attitudes contribute to the problem in today's pulpits. As we share their findings, we will also attempt to draw some applications:

1. Like other adults, many leaders struggle with personal relationships. Being a spiritual leader of people creates unusual relational dynamics and expectations. One of the results is often a lost sense of connection with others: a majority of pastors (61%) admit that they "have few close friends."

One pastor's wife that we ministered to said, "We are completely isolated and cut off from others. We have no support."

One-sixth of today's pastors feel under-appreciated. Pastors also deal with personal family problems: one in every five contends

24

that they are currently "dealing with a very difficult family situation."

Part of the problem here is that if a pastor shares his struggles with other leaders in his church, he runs the risk of rejection or being accused of not being worthy of his high calling. Or they may share his weaknesses with others in the congregation resulting in shame or a loss of respect. When a leader attempts to share his personal problems with his peers in the community, he runs the risk of being shunned or isolated. Pastors often feel that there really is nowhere for them to turn.

I remember once when our daughter was struggling in her teen years. In our desire to be transparent leaders we asked our congregation for prayer. It was a beautiful time as we prayed and took communion on her behalf in one of our services. Everyone seemed so supportive. It wasn't until a few years later when some accusations were being stirred up against us that those same people cited the Biblical charge from 1 Tim. 3 saying, "A leader must manage his own household well…. If a man is unable to manage his own household, how will he manage the household of God?" What had been a beautiful expression of love and support in the congregation, down the road was used as a weapon against us by mean-hearted individuals.

2. Most pastors are supremely confident in their abilities to teach, make disciples and lead. Pastors express the greatest degree of confidence in their capability as "effective Bible teachers" -- 98% of pastors said this phrase accurately described them. More than nine out of every ten pastors also feel that they are "effective leaders" and a similar proportion believes they are "driven by a clear sense of vision."

More than eight out of ten claims to be an "effective disciple maker." Another favorable perception maintained by pastors is that they are "deeply involved in the community," a label embraced by seven out of ten leaders.

These statistics amaze me. Why? Because - *If* their perceptions were actually true, it stands to reason that the destructive calamity in today's churches would be far less. In other words, if pastors are *so effective* at leading, discipling, and casting vision, why are the wheels coming off the wagon? Why is there so much misunderstanding and accusation? Why are so many congregations not on the same page with their leaders? Perhaps leaders aren't as capable as they think they are. There may be a huge disconnect between what leaders believe about their ministry skills and how they are actually viewed. And of course, there can also be agitators in the church who aren't happy no matter how effective the leader is.

3. Many leaders depict their personalities as shy and introverted. Despite the interpersonal demands of congregational ministry, one-quarter of the nation's senior pastors describe themselves as introverts (24%). This is the same proportion as in the general adult population (25%) and suggests that church work is not merely for those drawn to the limelight. Still, the research also revealed that introverted leaders are more likely to feel under-appreciated in ministry and are more apt to feel relationally isolated.

Not being an introvert, I have often found myself wishing I was one. These amazing leaders seemed to have the gift of genuinely listening and showing compassion to those they ministered to. Their quiet manner and understanding way seemed so *pastoral.* Although my preaching was always centered on the Scriptures, my style was fun, energetic, lively and encouraging. Perhaps we could liken my sermons to a Biblical *Tonight Show* monologue.

But did you catch the part about feeling under-appreciated and relationally isolated? When I read this, I thought of presidential candidate Ben Carson. What an amazingly gifted man. Smart, articulate, a compassionate man, full of wisdom and with a moral compass. And yet, I believe his quiet demeanor had a lot to do with people not wanting him to lead the country. I heard people say about him, "If you're going to lead -- lead!" I wonder if this same problem happens in our churches today with introverted leaders?

4. Risk-taking drops off among pastors after 20-plus years in ministry. Taking appropriate and calculated risks is an important attribute among leaders and most pastors consider themselves to be risk-takers. But the research shows that the risk-taking impulse declines significantly after someone has been a pastor for 20 or more years. Pastors who have stayed at the same church for more than 20 years are particularly "risk averse."

Church leaders must be people of vision, and be willing to share that vision with the church. Jesus said, "The Kingdom of God suffers violence and the violent take it by force," (Matt. 11:12). I'm not sure what that means in its totality, but it certainly involves risk taking. Stagnation and keeping the status quo will never accomplish Kingdom purposes. This statistic also highlights one of the age-old problems: *Inexperienced* pastors tend to run after the vision without the wisdom to navigate rough waters. And, about the time they gain enough wisdom to lead the church into deeper waters, they decide to play it safe.

5. Despite portrayals of pastors being single-minded in their focus on ministry, most pastors feel they lead a balanced life. Like many adults, church leaders have difficulty putting good intentions into practice. Most pastors say they try hard to stay healthy and have a wide range of interests, even while dealing with an array of intense occupational pressures and expectations.

The truth is that most pastors are consumed with the ministry and run the risk of burnout. With few friends, a lack of extra finances, and little time to pursue other interests, too often pastors do not join gyms, get out to social events, join clubs or have interests outside of the church to help relieve stress and bring balance. In the long run, this can be very costly to the leader and to the congregation.

6. The age of the leader often influences self-perceptions. It seems as if both generational distinctions and life experience affect how pastors think of themselves. For instance, Boomer leaders (those ages 45-70) were most likely to say they have few close friends, but they were the least likely to feel under-appreciated. Older pastors (ages 70+) were the most likely to feel inadequately recognized for their efforts. Introversion was most common among Buster pastors (ages 25-45), but young leaders were also the most likely to perceive themselves as risk-takers. True to their friendship-oriented generational identity, Buster pastors were also the least likely to feel relationally isolated even if they are introverts.

The issue here is self-perception versus reality. Now in my mid 60's, I have seen many of my friends go through what is commonly called a mid-life crisis. This usually looks something like an old guy getting some tattoos or earrings, buying a motorcycle, none of my friends can afford a sports car and dressing like a hippie. (If that's REALLY you, please forgive the analogy). The Scriptures tell us to "not think more highly of ourselves than we should" Romans 12:3. This verse is not just about pride, but it is the ability to take an honest assessment of ourselves, to know our strengths, weaknesses, gifts, and talents, and out of this true assessment bring others on to the team who make up for our weaknesses. Yes, humility is a big part of this one.

Looking at these statistics helps us to see more clearly the complexities and inner struggles that pastors and leaders grapple with. Add this to the demands that congregations put on pastors and we can see that the stress levels of ministry are very high.

Leaders often feel stuck in the middle of two conflicting tensions. They have the desire to lead definitively and speak the uncompromising Word of the Lord, but people do not always want to hear those convicting messages or be led that strongly. It seems everyone has become an expert on truth and how best to lead a congregation.

God Breaks In But Not Everyone Is Happy

I'll never forget the Sunday when the Presence of the Lord seemed significantly more evident than usual. From the time the first note of worship was sung, it was clear that God was *up to something*. On that particular Sunday, we never did get to the sermon, the announcements, or the offering for that matter. People were being touched and it was a beautiful move of God.

But the really confusing thing happened immediately after the service. I had just barely reached my office when a couple, who had been a part of the church for many years, appeared in the doorway. "We are grateful for such a precious move of God today," they began. "Had this not happened, it would have been our last service here, Pastor. We were planning on leaving the church. But now we are staying."

After they walked out, I had a moment to thank God and was grateful to Him as I had little to do with what had taken place. But my thoughts were cut short when another couple walked through my office door. "Pastor," they began, "If we ever have another service like we did today, we are leaving the church. We came here to hear the Word of God, not to have some emotional sing-a-long with no structure." As quickly as they walked in, they walked out.

WOW! I thought to myself, *Were these two couples in the same service?* As a leader, how can you lead such a diverse group? But that's the tension in the church today. Everyone seems to be an expert on how to lead a church, how to grow a church, what music should be played, what should be preached and the direction the service should go. I get stressed out just writing about it! This tension in leading happens to so many pastors, on so many levels.

Many pastors live in fear

One local pastor, we knew quite well had been in his denomination for 35 years. He told me that he was reluctant to address the way his denomination was embracing homosexual lifestyles because he was afraid of being put out of the denomination and couldn't afford to lose his pension. Other pastors have indicated that if they were uncompromising in their messages it would result in dissension in the church or the loss of members and finances.

The Fuller Institute, with George Barna, cited that the number one reason that pastors leave the ministry is that "Church people are not willing to go the same direction or embrace the goals of the pastor. Pastors believe the Lord is leading them to go in one direction, but the people are not willing to follow or change." One pastor recently told me that in the aftermath of a congregational meeting, his church went from 1100 members to 400 members almost overnight because of a decision he had made to move the church in a direction allowing for what he called "a greater freedom of the Spirit."

In addition to so many pastors and their families being wounded in ministry, the church is negatively impacted as well. Over 7,000 churches close their doors annually in America and as was said earlier, of those churches that remain open, many struggle for decades trying to recover. Years ago, we were in a meeting where Bob Mumford was speaking to pastors about the challenge of leading today's churches. He said, "The church is almost un-pastorable." I had been in the ministry for just a short time, so I was shocked, to say the least. But our experience and our findings from other church leaders have all too often confirmed this sad statement.

Having been through all that we have, I've tried to sort out the real underlying issues and not just focus on the immediate situation. You see, if we remain focused on people, we may never get at what is really important. Let's face it, people are fickle. "Armchair Quarterbacks" have been around for a long time. Everyone has become an *expert* on almost *everything*. Don't believe me? Check out the endless arguments on Facebook. As someone said, "Opinions are like elbows, everyone has at least two of them."

I remember the time a man in his late 40's came into my office to "tell me how to best run the church." And although I have always wanted to have input from people of all ages, he didn't come with suggestions -- he came with a mandate. He proceeded to tell me what we should be doing more of and how best to do it. He spent the next five minutes arguing his points. (Did you ever find out that there are some people who want the privilege of leading the church without carrying the responsibilities of leading it?) Having already had a long day, I must confess that I probably didn't have a lot of patience. After listening to his litany of plans and directions, (I wanted to hear him out in case he actually did have some good points), I asked him if he had ever been to Bible school? "No," he replied. "Well, how about seminary?" His answer again was "No." "Have you ever taken any church leadership courses or church growth seminars?" Again, he answered, "No." I then asked him what he did for a living? He told me that he was a plumber. I then told him that I knew NOTHING about plumbing. At that moment, I don't know if it was righteous anger or listening to the devil, but that's when I let him have it.

I asked, "Well, sir, how would you feel if I came on your job site and began telling you how to run the pipes, fix the drain lines, or put in the fixtures?" He told me that he wouldn't like it because I had no clue what I was talking about. I responded, "You have a lot of nerve coming into my office to tell me how to lead this church when you have no clue what you're talking about. You didn't come in with any positive suggestions on moving forward, you came only to criticize what we are doing and tell us how to implement your plans without even understanding why we're doing what we're doing." Honestly, I was secretly hoping that the Lord was calling him to a different church. So much for the advice of "experts." In his book, *When Sheep Attack,* Dennis Maynard says, "We are dealing with a generation that believes they are the authorities in all areas despite the fact that they have no training or experience."

We've Got Your Back

I always believed that the brothers and sisters who you were affiliated with would have your back in a crisis. After all, these are the people who have probably known you the longest. Perhaps you went to their Bible school or college. Most likely you interviewed with them to receive your credentials. They have seen the fruit of your ministry in previous locations. You attend their reunions and further study programs. And, you usually give a portion of your tithe to them. So, when the antagonists begin to accelerate their attacks and take it to the overseers, why does the denomination, in most cases, seem to believe the opposition?

In the case study of churches that had fired their pastors, Dennis Maynard reports that each congregation had experienced an increase in attendance and financial giving. Likewise, there was an air of excitement with increased activity at church events until the conflict began. Every congregation was alive and growing at the time the antagonists accelerated their attacks against the pastor. And when the attacks came, the pastors reported that the overseers "almost immediately sided with the antagonists." They reported that their bishops actively worked with the antagonists for their removal. Some of them turned on the pastors completely, attacking them verbally, sending them for psychological evaluation, investigating their past ministries and threatening to "defrock" them as being unfit for ministry. In each case, the denominational leaders chose to believe the dissenters and remove the pastor.

One pastor shared that when he was fired, he was in shock. It had just been a week before that he had received a glowing report on his evaluation. The church was really doing well – it was growing and the spirit was good. One of the elders came to him on Christmas Eve and told him he needed to resign that coming Sunday. The pastor was told that he couldn't say anything about it or he would not receive severance pay. The entire church was in shock because the pastor couldn't tell anyone why he was resigning. So, he resigned and left town, without giving an explanation.

Another leader reported, "I didn't even know that my Bishop was involved until I received a telephone call from him. He just started shouting at me over the telephone. He was blaming me for all the problems in the church." Another pastor wrote, "He didn't even ask me for my point of view. He assumed everything that the antagonists had told him about me was true." At first glance, one would think that a pastor under attack by a handful of dissidents needs only call the denominational office and the appropriate authority would come to the rescue. Our study has dispelled that notion.

Getting To The Heart Of The Matter

After leaders go through a church crisis (large or small), we tend to spend a lot of time analyzing the situation over and over again. *Who did what? Who said what? What did they mean by that? Why did they say it?* We can only try to understand their motives, the politics involved, or how they manipulated others to achieve their goals. But all of this is just smoke. The truth is that it's hard to figure people out.

The real underlying issues that church leaders need to grapple with are contained in questions like Where was God in all of this? What was God doing? Did He abandon me in my hour of need? Did God have a plan, for my good, during this crisis? Does God even care? This is the meat of it. These are the real issues. You see, we all know that people can and will let us down but how tormented is the man who believes that God has let him down in his hour of need. If you are able to find answers to *these* questions, you'll be able to find rest for your soul and lay your anger down. This is the place that we want to go next. This is the place you will find healing and restoration.

CHAPTER THREE

Where Was God During My Crisis?

One of the most frequent questions that leaders ask when they go through a devastating trial in their church is "Where was God during all this?" We know that people can be un-Christ-like. Let's face it, they can be downright vicious. The accusations never seem to stop. Some may even lie. The unpleasant truth is that people *will* fail you. But what about God? Why does it seem like He failed us, too? I found myself flopping in my bed at 3:00 a.m. wondering, *Doesn't He care? Is He powerless to stop my former friends from hurting me and my family? Why would He allow Satan to have a victory that leaves a church in disarray and leaders wounded almost beyond endurance?*

It seems so contrary to His will and the furthering of the Kingdom. The thought has crossed my mind, *Perhaps God likes it when I suffer.* I've got to admit that I've felt like Jim Carrey in the comedy movie, *Bruce Almighty.*

39

After losing his job, his marriage and having the rest of his life seemingly fall apart, Bruce begins letting God, (played by Morgan Freeman), have it with both barrels. "God is a mean kid with a magnifying glass. The only One around here not doing His job is You. Smite me, oh mighty Smiter." Then he puts the cherry on top by saying to His face, "You suck!"

Now I'm sure *you've* probably never really said any of those things to God (like I have). But when you're at the bottom looking up through all the layers of apparent injustice, it just might be possible that you've had a few thoughts along these lines.

Let me make this statement to get it out there. We'll look at it in more detail later. The statement is this: At some point in the midst of our pain, we're probably going to ask the question, Is God really against me? My answer to that is, I don't think so. I believe that He loves you and agonizes right along with you in the crises. He is not doing this *to* you. He is totally with you, but He is working through the brokenness of this world to accomplish something greater in you and in those around you.

During my hours of nocturnal pondering, I too came to the question "Where was God in this?" This is the question of the hour. Why? Because nothing else will make sense if we don't understand how God could let this happen and understand what He was doing in our lives through it all. Therefore, this chapter is the most important of all the chapters of this book.

Sorting It All Out

Other common questions pastors ask during a crisis are "Who needs this?" "If this is what the ministry is like, why would anyone want to do it?" And deeper still, "Why would the God of love call me to do this and then allow me and my family (not to mention the church) go through this?" It's unanswered questions like these that open the door to anger and bitterness -- and not just toward people or the church, but toward the Lord Himself. Why does God allow trauma to impact quality men and women who love the Lord and have sacrificed themselves to serve Him?

David Goetz said it well. "Few people understand what it's like to be constantly bombarded with criticisms and rarely encouraged or thanked. It needs to be said that churches simply don't know how to love pastors. They really don't trust them to make long-term decisions for the betterment of the church. They want leaders, but as soon as they get them, they have a compulsion to bring them down."

The question is as old as the scriptures. Why did the Lord allow Joseph to be betrayed by his brothers, sold into slavery and put in prison for 14 years based on false accusation, (Gen. 37)? Why did God allow David to be anointed king and yet have to flee for his life, hiding in caves from a jealous, demonized man, (1 Sam. 18:10)? Why did Elijah have to run for his life from Jezebel's wrath when he was in the right, (1 Kings 19:2)? Why was Paul put in a basket and lowered over the wall for fear of death, followed by years in the wilderness, (Acts 9:25)? In the musical *Fiddler On The Roof*, when trying to figure out why all this trouble was happening, Tevye says to God, "I know, I know, we are your Chosen People. But once in a while couldn't You choose someone else?" None of us is alone in asking that question.

False Accusations Abound

After doing a case study with 25 ministers who were fired from their churches, David Maynard found a pattern. "Not one single case had any of the clergy done anything that would have been considered criminal in a court of law. By the same token, none of them had done anything that would bring them before an ecclesiastical court for discipline. While none had done anything criminal and none were subjected to canonical discipline, rumors filled with innuendo and accusation with haunt some of them for the rest of their ministries." Maynard adds; "Many pastors say; 'I still don't know what I did wrong. Everything was going so well...Please somebody tell me what I did wrong.'" (*When Sheep Attack*)

When we went through our crisis, having been rejected by our church, our denomination, and our community, we were angry, and we began to question everything. To say that we were shaken to our foundation would be quite accurate. We questioned our beliefs, our theology, and our faith. Things that we had been taught and presumed to be true, were now suspect. We questioned our leaders. We questioned our relationships. We questioned our calling. And, we questioned God.

Playing Chess On Multiple Levels

When describing what the Lord is doing in the earth, Mike Bickle often says that "God plays chess on multiple levels at once." So when we begin to try and answer the question, "Where was God in all of this?" or, "Why would God let this happen?" it would be presumptuous for us to think we could identify all that God was doing in our lives, but also in His people, the community, and the denomination during our crisis. But one thing was certain; God *was* working in our lives through it all, for our good and His glory, and He *is* working in your life as well. His leadership is perfect, and He never wastes an opportunity to work His grace and character into us. This might not feel like a true statement to you, but don't bail on me yet.

God plays chess on multiple levels at the same time

At this writing, we are 25 years out from the experience we had with our church. The years have brought some healing and perspective that we lacked when we were caught in the middle of that whirlwind that was sucking the life out of us. There's a common saying that "Time heals all wounds." I would say yes and no. We all know people who are still hurting and perhaps even complaining about an injustice that happened years ago. Time by itself doesn't heal -- but processing plus appropriate grief plus time can heal wounds, although, like Israel, we will probably always walk with a limp.

For months I thought, *even God can't make this disaster into something good!* If I'd gotten a tattoo during that time it would have been "Romans 8:28" with a slash through it. I even felt like He should have left it out of the Bible. But I must admit that looking back through those 25 years, Michelle and I can see so many ways that God did use this horrendous experience for our good. We hope that as you read from the middle of your whirlwind that you will be encouraged by the healing and growth that God brought to us through ours.

So Let's Get To It: What Was God Doing?

Here are some things we feel the Lord may address during a crisis in ministry.

1. Dealing With Pride (What do You mean, "I'm not the next Charles Spurgeon?")

Perhaps the first thing He was doing was dealing with pride in our hearts. Now please don't tear the book up yet. If your situation was like ours, many of those who brought accusation and faultfinding were completely un-Christ-like and carnal; some even resorted to lies, gossip, and slander and we did not deserve what they did to us, and perhaps you didn't either. Many of our accusers followed the same patterns of those who falsely accused the Lord and the saints down through the centuries. They are, as the Apostle Paul put it, "enemies of the cross," (Phil. 3:18). At the same time, it would be presumptuous for us to say that all our words and actions were totally Christ-like.

Though Jesus was falsely accused, He kept His heart right and "opened not His mouth" Acts 8:32. We didn't always keep our

45

hearts right, and at times, I'm sorry to say, we didn't keep our mouths shut. No, we didn't take out an ad in the New York Times, but it took little prodding from friends who inquired "What did they do to you?" for us to regurgitate all the gory details. At times our hearts were full of hatred and it sometimes came out as we shared. Of course, having worked with many church leaders I now understand that it is critically important to have a place to share honestly and openly without the fear of some kind of judgment. Everyone needs at least one person to help process the pain. Wounds need to get cleaned out before healing can take place.

Now getting back to this issue of pride.... We were surprised by point number two in the previous chapter that most pastors are *supremely confident* in their abilities to teach, make disciples, and lead. (italics mine). Pastors express the *greatest degree of confidence* in their capability as an "effective Bible teacher" (98% of pastors said this phrase accurately described them). More than nine out of every ten pastors also feel that they are an *effective leader* and a similar proportion believe they are *driven by a clear sense of vision*. I would have been the first to smugly agree with those statements. I prided myself on my anointed teachings. I had also raised up an excellent group of men and women -- potential leaders that we were discipling. We had a great vision with a wonderful flowchart to prove it.

So, let's get this straight. As a pastor, I have *supreme confidence* that I am an effective teacher, leader, and disciple maker and I have a clear vision. So, if there is any problem in the church, any misunderstanding, any miscommunication or disagreement, it couldn't possibly be me – it *has to be them.* Brothers and sisters, it pains me to say it, but this is nothing less than pride. We may never verbalize it, but in our hearts, we are asking, *"What's wrong with them, don't they know that my leadership is amazing?"* May I remind you that God resists the proud? Prov. 3:34. Again, this is not an excuse for accusations and wrong behavior on the part of anyone attacking leaders. It is also not necessarily the cause for why the crisis happened in the first place. It is, however, *one* of the things that the Lord puts His finger on during the process of playing chess on multiple levels. He uses the circumstances to reveal our hearts so that we might humbly repent of pride, turn to Him and be changed.

How Does God Deal With Pride?

Let's take a few minutes and look a little more closely on how God deals with pride. You see, both pride and humility are attitudes or responses of our will. We are free to respond with whichever attitude we want.

47

This is an area of free will, or what the Bible sometimes calls *the heart*. For example, if someone has the skill to play a musical instrument well, they can do so with a heart of pride or one of humility. It's their choice. Skill and attitude are different, and none of us can tolerate a person spewing out how wonderful they are.

Pride is the wrong response that we choose to have in any area of skill/strength. Strengths can include things like our good looks, financial status, the size of our ministry, our communication skills, a particular talent, our position in a denomination or any other area of success. And even though someone may work hard to fine-tune and improve their skills, they are still God-given. All praise belongs to Him. The Lord will *not* allow us to keep an attitude of pride about a skill set that He has given us in the first place. "I just got the lead in the Easter cantata" makes everyone a little nauseous.

Here's the amazing thing. The Biblical principle found throughout the Scriptures is that the Lord *has given mankind free will*. The freedom to choose goes all the way back to the garden of Eden. We have the freedom to choose humility or pride. So, when our will is contrary to clear Scriptural truths, He honors our free will. So then, how does He deal with our pride? The answer is *He deals with the strength or skill that we have placed our pride in until we wake up and recognize that we have made the wrong choice -- that of pride.* God messes with our strengths in order to deal with our attitudes.

Let me illustrate using a couple of Biblical examples. We'll start with Moses and then move to every pastor's favorite -- Peter.

The first few chapters of Exodus relate how Moses grew up in Pharaoh's courts, raised as the son of Pharaoh's daughter. His position as a member of the royal family would have given him access to education in history, philosophy, training in leadership and perhaps even instruction in military strategy. His life was clearly favored. His leadership, accomplishments, and position were his strengths -- strengths that the Lord bestowed upon him. How did Moses respond? Pride! He began to see himself as the savior of the downtrodden Israelites. This was his true calling, but the Lord would never allow him to serve in that position with an attitude of pride. When Moses saw the injustices laid upon the Israelites, his pride caused him to think that he could save them. Rising up, he killed an Egyptian. In His faithfulness, the Lord resists Moses' pride -- not by dealing directly with it, for this would be a violation of Moses' will. Instead, the Lord dealt with the strengths that Moses' pride was based on. God allowed the wheels to fall off the wagon and Moses found himself stripped of his title and his position, cast out of Egypt and tending sheep in the wilderness for 40 years.

Wow! Talk about touching his strengths! There is no place for pride in this demotion. In fact, years later, when the Lord finally called Moses to set His people free, Moses' saw himself as bankrupt. Because his strengths had been stripped, his former pride was now replaced with humility. Moses didn't even want the job. He argued that he was unable to accomplish the task. "What will I say; I'm not able to even speak," (Ex. 4:10). There is no longer any grasping or striving; that has been worked out of him. The Lord resisted Moses' pride by dealing with his strengths.

Perhaps you can relate to Moses' story. Although I knew this principle well, I still thought the success of our church had something to do with me. Duh! Yes, I had some skills that I even refined and disciplined so that I could be the best leader possible, but any pride that I had was the wrong response to God's gracious gifts in my life. Romans 9:16 says, "For it does not depend on the man who wills or the man who runs, but on God who has mercy."

Peter is much the same. He was the disciple Jesus publicly called "The Rock." He holds the position of being one of the three disciples closest to Jesus. He is always mentioned first among the "big three." He was on the Mount of Transfiguration and let's not forget that he was the only one who got out of the boat and walked on the Sea of Galilee. His strengths are obvious, but unfortunately, his heart was filled with pride, instead of humility. His prominence among the twelve should have humbled him, but Peter chose to respond with pride instead. When Jesus announced at the Last Supper that one of the twelve would deny Him, Peter boldly stated that it wouldn't be him. After all, he was The Rock. In His mercy, the Father resisted Peter's pride -- not by violating Peter's will directly, but by dealing with the strength and the platform upon which Peter built the pride in his own heart. When Peter denied the Lord, three times, He became bankrupt. He was busted. He lost everything. The Rock had become The Rubble. He felt completely unworthy of being a disciple. His pride was gone, and he was filled with shame. In his brokenness, Peter quit the ministry. When Easter Sunday came, Jesus told the women to specifically tell Peter that He would meet with him in the upper room. Peter was so broken that he needed the Lord's personal invitation in his restoration process.

Can you relate? I can. I was one of the 9 out of 10 who had "supreme confidence" in my ability to lead and pastor. I read all the how-to books and strategically went about implementing them to cause our ministry to rapidly grow. How about you? How have you responded to the strengths of your life? How did you respond to God's favor in your ministry? What have you done with the compliments about your preaching, church growth, or miracles that have taken place? Publicly we may have given thanks and homage to God for His grace and favor, but what secret thoughts of self-accomplishment and pride have we held?

The crisis itself may be just the thing that the Lord is using to teach us humility and deal with our pride.

2. Helping Us Run After True Success

> Publicly we may have given thanks and homage to God for His grace and favor, but what secret thoughts of self-accomplishment and pride have we held?

I was on my way home from an area minister's meeting, where I had the privilege of meeting several fine pastors from our city. I was invited by a friend that I had known for some 30 years. He had also invited another pastor, Sam, whom I had never met. As we traveled home after the meeting Sam said, "I found it refreshing that no one asked me how big my church was." We all chuckled because in 35 years of ministry it has been my experience that within five minutes of talking to a pastor at a clergy meeting, the question will be asked; "So how many attend your church?" I love the standard response a friend of mine gives, "Our church is doing awesome -- it's dying slower than any church I've ever pastored."

As I said earlier, the ideologies of the western church have caused not only heartache but often appeal to the soulish heart of man. Our drive for what we consider success in the western *world* has also affected our understanding of success in the western *church*. There are scores of books on how to be a successful pastor, how to grow your church, how to double the offerings, how to double your attendance, and how to get people to serve. Many of these books may be valid as helpful tools in reaching people, but it's the motive of wanting to be the biggest, or the best, or the fastest growing in our city that seems to have more to do with our position and prominence and little to do with seeing lives genuinely touched by the power of the cross.

You may object by citing that the New Testament church exploded with first 3,000 and then 5,000, Acts 2:41 and 4:4. True. But the motive of the disciples wasn't to be big.

Their motive was a pure desire to see the Kingdom of God established. Growth was the natural outcome.

In more recent years, we have had the privilege of serving in a ministry where 75 % of those attending were young people, mostly in their 20's. When they are asked what they want to do in ministry, most of them give a response that indicates that they want to impact the world in a huge way. Wow! Of course, to them, this means that they want to fill stadiums or lead large ministries. Admittedly, when I was a young man just getting involved in the ministry that would have been my response as well. The truth is that when I said, "I want to reach our whole community for Christ" what I meant was, "I want to have a large ministry with lots of people and lots of resources, so I would be famous and be invited to travel the world and speak."

What is true success?
And, why do we want it?

Unfortunately, I was motivated more by my western beliefs of success than I was by the knowledge that lost people were going to Hell. To me, success had to do with large numbers, big buildings, and an equally big reputation. Of course, being rich wouldn't hurt either.

One young man in his first year of Bible School told me that he wanted to be the next Billy Graham. My question was, "Why?"

Don't get me wrong. We all want success and the Lord wants us to be successful. Success is not contrary to God's will or Word. Let's face it, the church of the first century was successful by any standard and experienced miraculous growth on a regular basis. God is obviously not afraid of church growth, large numbers or someone having a reputation. After all, "Saul slew his thousands, but David his ten thousands," (1 Sam. 18:7)

But is success always equal to church growth? Is a pastor unsuccessful if in his course of ministry, he only has 50 members but shepherds them well? Is the missionary who lays his life down for years in another country, ministering to just 20 people unsuccessful? How should we define success? Are we to assume that our western standard of success is the right one for leading a church? How does God define success? As I said, in western cultures, success almost *always* means bigger. The issue here is the motive of the heart -- not the numbers, the size, the buildings, or the offerings.

True Success

In the Gospels, Jesus makes no distinction between the success of the faithful steward who was rewarded with one more talent and the steward who received five more talents. Both were told, "Well done good and faithful servant," (Matt. 25:21, 23). They were both successful. What God is looking for is *faithfulness in what we have been given.* True success is about faithfulness in serving God regardless of size, fame or notoriety. In 2 Cor. 10:13, Paul says that each of us has been given a sphere and a measure. He then encourages us to understand our sphere and work within it. Not everyone is called to have a worldwide ministry. And just because we attend the right conference or read the right book doesn't mean that we are now equipped to do so.

Remember when Moses was raising up a leadership team to help him pastor the millions in the wilderness? He placed some over tens, some over fifties and some over hundreds. Why? Because God designed each of them with a capacity of service. It begs the questions: Were the ones who oversaw the tens able to grow to fifties with the right church growth manual? Were the ones with the hundreds considered more successful than the ones placed over ten or fifty? Did the leaders of larger groups look down their noses at the ones with smaller groups? You see, when we stand before the throne of God, the question will never be "How big did your church grow?" It will be "Where you faithful with what I gave you?" And in that day, the only thing our hearts will rejoice in hearing will be; "Well done *good and faithful* servant, enter into the joy of your master". This is the true success that must motivate our hearts at every level of ministry.

For years I strove to have a church of thousands while the Lord was only interested in my faithfulness with hundreds. While the Lord was looking at me as His faithful servant, I was begrudging the numbers I had, always wanting more. At this writing, I have the joy of overseeing a home group of about 16. And on a side note, together we are experiencing more of what I would call New Testament church life with the 16 people than we did in many of our larger church experiences. I'm learning to just be faithful with what the Lord has given me today. As Clint Eastwood says in one of the *Dirty Harry* movies; "A man's got to know his limitations." How true.

Okay, so God may be dealing with our pride and our definition of success during a crisis. But let's take this a step deeper.

3. Helping Us Find Our Identity and Worth

Not only have many leaders in the Body of Christ confused success with numbers, but many in church leadership have mistakenly linked their *identity and worth* with outward accomplishments, possessions or numbers.

It's not just that we want a large ministry; it's that we feel like failures until we have one.

First, let me say that your worth has never been, nor will it ever be, connected to accomplishment. I know pastors who for years tried to live up to what they believed to be their Heavenly Father's expectations because they never got their earthly father's approval. They now strive to gain God's approval with large numbers or other standards of success -- hoping that their Heavenly Father will be proud of them. The truth is, our identity and worth are based solely on the fact that God chose us and loves us. He pursued us, even when we were His enemies, and adopted us into His family. Our value and worth are based on His choice of us, not our offerings and sacrifices that we present to Him. Having three fantastic children and seven beautiful grandchildren, I can assure you that none of them ever did anything to be worthy of all my love, approval, and acceptance. I love them because they're mine.

When the reality of God's unconditional acceptance hit my soul and I realized that I didn't have to "prove myself" anymore, I wept. I realized that I had created a mental image of how I should be and what I should accomplish. It was a goal that I could never achieve, and it led to a constant inner feeling of failure. It kept moving further and further away with every level of success I did reach. That's because the standard of *being successful* was a wound in my own heart that had to be healed, and no amount of success would be good enough until the healing came. It was through our church crisis when I felt that I was an utter failure, at my lowest place, that I finally felt fully accepted and loved by our Father. With that revelation, I was able to be completely healed.

4. Sorting Out the Confusion Between Assignment and Relationship

A survey of pastors found that 72% only studied the Bible when they were preparing for sermons or lessons. This left only 38% who read the Bible for relationship with God and personal devotion. To me, this is one indicator that too many pastors are focused on their ministry assignment and not their relationship with the Lord.

A pastor friend of ours has a large ministry which impacts people all over the world. Thousands attend his ministry and tens of thousands come for his annual conference. Recently when looking at the fruit of his labors, someone said to him, "Wow, your dream is finally coming to pass." To which our friend responded, "No, my ministry is my assignment -- not my dream. The dream of my heart is simply to love the Lord because He loves me, and to grow in that reality."

When he shared that, I was cut to the heart because I realized that I spent years in ministry focusing on my assignment rather than my relationship. Ministry assignment and relationship are two different things. Whether large or small, our ministry is our assignment -- to which we should be faithful -- but it should never be our dream. And it certainly is not the same as our love relationship with God. At the beginning of our church crisis, my focus was more on my assignment. It was only through the process of the crisis that I began to refocus more on my relationship with the Father. The Lord used the crisis to bring me back into relationship with Him. Sometimes it takes the failure of an assignment to see the importance of relationship.

John Eldridge often challenges men to "live out of their heart." In other words, live out your dreams. John shares that too many men spend most of their lives doing everything but that. Sometimes we feel bound to work at jobs that we hate. We may feel stuck in lives that we do not want. For those of us who are called to ministry, may I suggest that our calling is actually to the Lord Himself, not just a position of leadership in the church? He is the One to whom we are called. In Psalm 27:4, David says "One thing I have asked of the Lord and that I shall seek...to behold the beauty of the Lord and to inquire in His temple." Remember, the priests of Old

Covenant did not inherit a portion of the land, for the Lord, Himself was their inheritance. Deuteronomy 18:2

Only when we pursue our relationship with God *first* will we truly be able to accomplish our *assignment* in a healthy, balanced way. Putting our assignment first will always lead to frustration. The Apostle Paul prayed that "we might know the breadth, length, height, and depth of the love of God," (Eph. 3:18). That to me sums up our relational goal. Of course, Paul knew his assignment from the Lord and was faithful to finish his course but that was altogether different than his relational pursuit of knowing Jesus.

Are you beginning to see how the Lord played chess on several levels with us? He never wastes an opportunity to take us deeper in our walk with Him. Let's look at a few more chess moves that the Lord made with us and could be making during your crisis.

5. Gaining a Deeper Understanding of Our Primary Calling

Now that we've seen the difference between our assignment and our relationship to the Lord, let's see how our relationship to God -- our "why" takes priority over our day-to-day "what." Asked what their calling is, most leaders respond by saying things like,

"I'm called to teach the word." "I lead worship." "I have a ministry to feed the homeless," or something similar. These may be true, but they are not our *primary* calling. There are three basic callings in the life of every believer; our *primary* or internal calling; our *secondary* or external calling, and thirdly, our *eternal* calling. Loving the Lord with all our heart, soul, mind and strength is our primary calling. That's it! Jesus called it the "great and foremost commandment," (Matt. 22:38) In other words, our primary calling is to be loved by God and to be lovers of God. This is true for every believer -- including church leaders. Our secondary calling is the assignment that the Lord has given us, whatever our vocation. Bricklayers, teachers, nurses, florists, and truck drivers all have an assignment from God. Thirdly, our eternal calling is that which we will be doing throughout eternity. (I trust you didn't think we were going to just sit around on clouds playing harps.)

It is amazing to me how much pressure the church places on senior pastors to be CEO's, as well as excellent preachers, visitation ministers, crisis counselors, or administrative directors. Staying focused on our primary calling -- to be loved by and a lover of God takes real effort. The driving force that every church leader must have is to understand why they are doing what they are doing. If we forget that our why is first and foremost to be a lover of God, then in time, ministry becomes just a job. Perhaps this is one of the reasons why so many pastors and leaders struggle with burnout, depression, and even suicide. One of the works of grace that God does in our hearts during a trial is to bring us back to the first commandment; back to our first love. It's too easy for pastors to allow our secondary calling (our ministry assignment) to take priority in our lives. This could explain the statistic about leaders studying the Word but doing it only for sermon preparation; their primary calling to Him has taken a backseat to service. One of the prophetic promises that we have heard over the past few years is that God was going to "restore the first commandment to first place" in the church. He is doing this in His leaders, and He does it really well during trials. Perhaps this is because trials have the potential to shake us to the core, out of our *busy routines* and refocus us on the Lord to find out what the heck is happening to us!

Let's look at one last thought before we move on. I believe that the Lord also uses trials to help clarify the difference between the "machinery of ministry" and the church as being the place where people encounter the living God. And because too many pastors are focused on reaching people, rather than encountering God, we have become builders of great programs instead of encountering His great presence.

Programs, outreaches, events, and worship (that is more like a concert, including laser lights and smoke machines), may help the church run, may have people saying "wow" about our services, and may even bring more people through the doors - but to what end – if we miss the opportunity to touch the hem of His garment? I'm not saying that organization, or programs or a good worship team are bad. What I'm saying is that we have settled for them as the major attraction rather than pointing people to an encounter with our awesome God. Remember, Jesus came to introduce us to the Father. John 17 That's the Good News, in fact, it's GREAT News! It's an encounter with Him that changes our lives, that heals our hurts, that sets men free. Some programs and organization may be needed to accomplish this, but encountering God is what makes the church different from every other place on earth. We must remember that organization and programs are the scaffolding that supports our real purpose—encountering Him.

> The Sunday morning *production* is amazing to say the least, and we attract people by the hundreds and thousands to see the show.

Years ago, I heard the story of a craftsman in the old country who built a windmill. Now, this was no ordinary windmill -- it was a work of art. It's size, beauty and artistry were the talk of the town. As word got out, people from all over the countryside came to spend the day picnicking beneath the grandeur of its sweeping arms. The problem was, there were days when the wind wasn't blowing. The old craftsman had an idea. He said, "I know, I'll put a small motor in the basement so that the windmill will be turning whether the wind is blowing or not." And so, he did, and everyone was happy. My friends, I believe this is the problem with the western church today. We have put a motor in the basement so that we no longer care if the wind of the Spirit is blowing or not in our services. We have built great churches with tons of organized ministries, programs, classes, and events. The Sunday morning *production* is amazing, to say the least, and we attract people by the hundreds and thousands to see the show.

Please don't get me wrong. I understand that without some organization and structure, the church will not move forward and genuine needs will be overlooked. Acts chapter six records just such an incident. The early church was growing at a miraculous rate, but the organization hadn't kept up. Before long some of the members were not being fed. The answer? Organize a group of men who would oversee this process and be sure all the needs were met. We need organization. But my own experience with pioneering and building several churches is that in time, administrating the organization we have built takes the place of our dependent relationship with the Lord and consumes time we could use to genuinely minister to the flock. The Apostle Paul reminded the Ephesian elders to "be on guard for yourselves and for all the flock, among which the Holy Spirit has made you overseers, to shepherd the church of God which He purchased with His own blood," (Acts 20:28).

Sadly, many church leaders are out of touch with the Lord and have lost sight of the people. The focus becomes more and more on *keeping the machinery running.* My concern is that in the church of today, far too much of the pastor's time is spent on keeping the machine well oiled. We have become spiritual CEOs more than shepherds of the flock. Do we really have too much *machinery* in place in our churches? Well, let's use the example of someone who wants to serve in one of the church's ministries. Somehow, we've put in place a number of hoops they must jump through in order to serve God in our church. They must go through six months of membership classes, then read nine books and memorize the church's core values. They must have perfect church attendance, and be approved by two elders. Oh, and let's not forget that they must be tithing. (The exaggeration is intentional). Of course, there is the place for training, discipleship and mentoring. But too often the *threshold to minister* is so high that it discourages or eliminates people who may have a genuine heart to serve.

A friend on Facebook recently made this very poignant statement about the Western Church. She said, "Christianity is dull and lifeless in this country. Because that's what the church leaders have done to it. They've made it into something so bland, so generic, and inoffensive that it no longer bears any resemblance to the faith of our Christian ancestors. Indeed, the primary goal of the modern church is to avoid offense at whatever cost."

I remember talking about the qualifications for eldership that one pastor was putting into place in his church. After reading through the steps, I said to him; "Pastor, the truth is that *you* wouldn't even qualify to be an elder in your own church with these requirements."

My observation is that too much of a pastor's time, money, energy, and efforts are focused on building all the machinery and then keeping it all running smoothly. We may call it "serving the Lord" but it isn't. Even the Apostles recognized that as senior leaders they needed to remain focused on the ministry of the Word; as they said in Acts 2:2, "It is not desirable for us to neglect the word of God in order to serve tables." The statistics cited earlier in this chapter showed that it is easy to spend 60 hours a week in the administrative, organizational issues of the church while neglecting the ministry of the Word and our relationship with the Lord. I believe this is at the very heart of one of the great failures of the western church. It seems a vicious circle. When our churches are too small to find enough volunteers to do the practical administration and run the programs, the pastor does it. As the church grows, one would think that these duties would be passed on to others. Instead, the demands of the machine seem to require the pastor to do even more administration. The church may one day grow large enough to have a church administrator on staff, but too often the senior pastor is still nothing more than a CEO.

> ## Getting an appointment with the pastor is like trying to get an audience with the Pope

I have seen large churches and ministries where the machinery is so big that the church is constantly asking for volunteers just to keep the machinery functioning. At that point the church is no longer about touching the lives of needy, hurting people; it has become an organizational monster. As the church grows, the machinery requires more and more time, money and staff to keep it running. Soon the leadership is asking every church member to volunteer for the *sake of the kingdom*. But whose kingdom? Obviously, some organization is needed to meet needs and avoid chaos; but the western church has gone way overboard in setting up and running programs while forgetting about cultivating a ministry that "seeks first the Kingdom."

Have you seen churches where the pastor is practically inaccessible to the congregation? He is escorted on and off the platform and whisked away through a side door. Getting an appointment with him is like trying to get an audience with the Pope.

Enough.

In His faithfulness, the Lord uses crises to bring us back to our first love. He doesn't seem to be bothered that the machinery of the organization is falling apart. He doesn't seem to care that the wheels are falling off the wagon. He's not worried about our reputation, size, ministries, budget and the many other things that comprise the bulk of the pastor's time and energy. He jealously desires His bride and wants first place in His church.

In his book *So You Don't Want To Go To Church Anymore,* Wayne Jacobsen does a superb job of addressing this problem in the western church. He says; "As long as we see church life as a meeting we'll miss its reality and its depth. If the truth were told, the Scriptures tell us very little about how the early church met. It tells us volumes about how they shared His life together. They didn't see the church as a meeting or an institution, but as a family living under the Father." He goes on to say, "The more organization you bring to church life, the less life it will contain." Wow. That's a powerful statement.

Besides dealing with any areas of pride, helping us realign our definitions of success, and getting our priorities in order, what else could God be doing through a crisis?

6. Crucifying Any Compromise

In the thrilling film *Clear and Present Danger,* Harrison Ford plays Jack Ryan, a CIA Deputy Director, who is investigating what seems to be a secret CIA operation assigned to take out a drug cartel in Columbia. When the operation goes sour and several members are killed, Ryan begins to suspect that his higher-ups in the CIA have masterminded the whole operation and left the men to die. As he digs deeper, he becomes aware that the President himself may be a part of the whole plot.

Ryan makes the decision to confront his colleagues with the evidence, regardless of the cost. Near the end of the movie, he stands in the Oval Office to confront the President directly. It doesn't get more intimidating than that. As Ryan presents the charges, the President berates him, "How dare you lecture me.... How dare you come in here and bark at me like some kind of junkyard dog!" This is the test! Will Ryan back down, compromise or water down the truth? No. His response to the President is "How dare you, sir!" And the following scene is Ryan sharing the facts before the Congress.

There is something in us that wants to be like Jack Ryan, or Dirty Harry, or Marshall Sam Gerard in *U.S. Marshals* who says at one point, "I don't bargain."

The sad reality is that there have been times when I have bargained, and you may have, too. When I realized that standing for the truth, or fighting for justice was going to cost me more than I cared to pay, I folded. The results: I withered like a Macy's Day balloon the day after the parade. I may only be able to count these cowardice times on one hand, but I believe that God is looking for men and women who "swear even to their own hurt,"

71

(NASV) or as the Message says; "Keep your word even when it costs you," (Psalm 15:4).

During our church crisis, I'm glad to say that this was one of the times that I stood for the truth. I threw caution to the wind and was completely honest. In fact, over the course of 35 years of pastoring, I can recall five huge situations where I spoke the truth without backing down. These were life-changing events with life-changing results. I wish I could tell you that in all five situations truth prevailed and I came out victorious, but no. In fact, in each instance, it cost me dearly. What was the cost? A position of Church Elder, the position of Internship Director and three times the position of Pastor to be exact. This doesn't include what it cost my family, my reputation, or my finances.

And for several years after the last incident, I felt like a failure. My reaction was not wanting to be in any type of leadership position. As I told Michelle, "At least then I couldn't get fired again." But in more recent days I have come to realize that winning isn't everything and having a position doesn't mean that you've succeeded. If by folding under the pressure, I had been able to maintain a title or receive a paycheck, then perhaps I'm just a hireling -- a term I could never stand to live with.

What often crystallizes during a conflict is whether or not we will be men and women who will not compromise -- no matter the cost.

7. Giving Us An Uncompromising Voice

In his book, *It's Not Business, It's Personal, my friend Bob Sorge lays out the purpose of leadership and ministry as seen through the eyes of John the Baptist as a friend of the bridegroom. He who has the bride is the bridegroom; but the friend of the bridegroom, who stands and hears him, rejoices greatly because of the bridegroom's voice. And so this joy of mine has been made full. He must increase, but I must decrease,"* (John 3:29-30)

As pastors and leaders, we serve in the role of friends of the bridegroom. Let's look at several key truths from this passage. First of all, notice that John is not called the friend of the bride but friend of the bridegroom. Church leaders are here to *serve* the bride in the absence of the bridegroom. They prepare her for the coming of the bridegroom -- on behalf of the bridegroom. Church leadership is not about the church, it is actually about Jesus. It is not about the people in our congregations, it's not about us and it is certainly not about properties or buildings. Our job is to help make the Church ready for Him.

Notice also that the friend of the bridegroom listens and hears the voice of the bridegroom and "rejoices greatly." Over my years in ministry, I'm sorry to say that I have taken joy from many things other than the voice of the bridegroom -- church growth, big offerings, and church transfer (both in and out). The Scriptures teach us that our joy is in hearing His voice - not hers (the church). I wish that I had understood this during my early years of pastoral ministry. Yes, I was taught to obey the Lord and desire to hear His voice, but I was also taught that if I wanted to be successful in ministry I needed to listen to the bride. I was encouraged to learn what she needed and try to meet those needs. As a good pastor, I was to care for the sheep which often times caused me to give in to her whims, and I certainly spent a lot of time listening to her complaints.

John points out that a friend of the bridegroom finds their true joy in hearing the voice of the bridegroom. When the bride is being more like Bridezilla, it is easy to try and make everyone happy. And even though we went into the ministry to serve the Lord and not to be a *man pleaser* the bride expected us to be servants of the church more than servants of the Lord. After all, they hired us. The results were that I spent many years in ministry trying to please the bride even though I didn't realize I was even doing it.

A friend of the bridegroom finds their true joy in hearing the voice

---

This trap has even deeper ramifications. As time goes on it is easy to go beyond just listening to the likes and dislikes of the bride. Out of our own need for approval, pastors can actually begin to set their affections on the bride. We can begin to live for her approval, her acceptance and her love.

- "Did she appreciate the sermon I gave?"

- "Does she appreciate the sacrifices that I make for her?"

- "I want to be careful not to offend her."

- "What message would she really get blessed by?"

Is it possible that many church leaders are focused more on her pleasure, rather than the Lord's pleasure?

What's even worse, if we do serve the bride well, she may begin to set her affections on us! I've heard these comments over the years;

- "Oh pastor, I just love when you pray, you are so anointed."

- "I enjoy guest speakers, but no one brings the Word with more power and authority than you."

- "Your wife is such a lucky woman. You are such a man of God."

If we allow our souls to feed on this rhetoric, we can be set up for a fall. How much easier my life would have been if I hadn't spent so much time trying to please the bride and win her affections. How much heartache would I have been spared if I hadn't been so concerned about the church liking me? I was not aware that out of my own insecurities I was chasing the affections of another man's betrothed.

Losing Your Voice and Reputation

In Matt. 3:3, John the Baptist calls himself, "the voice of one crying in the wilderness, to make ready the way of the Lord." One of the roles of the pastor is to clearly and accurately communicate the Word of the Lord. This needs to be done with grace and humility, but it must also be done without compromise. Jesus came speaking both grace and truth. Our job is to do nothing less. One of the unfortunate results of allowing the affections of the Bride to affect our hearts is that we metaphorically *lose our voice*. We lose the ability to be clear and uncompromising. We lose the ability to speak the mandates of the Scriptures and the principles that the Spirit of God has birthed in our hearts.

Here's how it works. As we run after the bride's affections, in time we become afraid that the bride will reject us, afraid that we may lose members, and afraid that the offerings will go down. This results in pastors who avoid speaking on the topics that they know should be addressed, in fear of the church's response. Too many pastors avoid addressing areas of compromise, laziness, carnality, and even sin in the church. Unlike John the Baptist who was "the voice of one crying," we lose our voice and speak on those topics that will tickle their ears. As we minister to the Body of Christ, there should be a place for a pat on the back but also for a swift kick in the butt.

The thing that preoccupies the hearts of many church leaders is the issue of reputation. Have you ever noticed that John the Baptist had very few things in the natural that attracted people to him? He wasn't worried about his reputation. Bob points out that here is a man who is doing his ministry in the wilderness rather than near a populated area where every church growth book would recommend. His diet and his clothing were offensive. Who wants to invite the pastor over for dinner when he eats locusts? Do you leave the legs on while cooking them? Furthermore, John's message was quite offensive. Perhaps if he was a bit more seeker sensitive and avoided phrases like "brood of vipers," (Luke 3:7), "the axe is laid at the root," (Matthew 3:10), "repent," (Matt. 3:10), and "He will burn up the chaff with unquenchable fire," (Luke 3:17), his sermons would have been a little more appealing.

Now I am not suggesting that these be our messages every Sunday. After all, we are messengers of the Good News. But we must have the freedom to speak the Word of the Lord with boldness when necessary. My point is this: There was nothing about John that was attractive in the natural. He was not worried about his reputation. Certainly, none of the young girls in the villages were running after this hairy mountain man. But today's pastors are doing all that they can to be the most attracting leaders they can be. We put our best foot forward to appear smart, well spoken, have a sense of humor, be deeply spiritual, appeal to all age groups, give clear leadership, be gracious, friendly and full of joy. God forbid that we offend anyone. My question is: Are we doing it for the bride or for the sake of the bridegroom?

Our desire to maintain a good reputation may be one of the things that the Lord deals with during our trial. Remember, Jesus "*made Himself* of no reputation," (Phil. 2:7 KJV). Wow, that is the exact opposite of what so many leaders try to do in today's Western church.

8. Bringing Us Into A Deeper Understanding Of God's Love Romans 8:1 "We know that all things work together for good to those who love God, to those who are called according to His purposes."

God has called us to have confidence in the face of trials. The problem is that gaining this confidence is a process that can only be learned during times of difficulty. In fact, He desires that we not only have confidence but that we have a deep sense of His never-ending love for us even in the very midst of trials. Amazingly, He is able to use trials to take us to a depth of maturity that we could otherwise never obtain.

Now don't get me wrong. Some of the things we go through are horrible. In no way can they be called *good*. In Romans 8:1, the apostle tells us that all things *work together* for good. It does not say that all things are good. My friend and mentor of many years, Paul Johansson, often tells the story of when he and his brother were young and snuck into the kitchen for some chocolate. Their mother was making a chocolate cake and the ingredients were on the counter. They spied a square of the chocolate and took it. As soon as they were out of sight they shoved the chocolate into their mouths, only to discover, "This tastes HORRIBLE!" It was unsweetened baker's chocolate. But we all know that the chocolate cake would taste horrible without the addition of that bitter tasting ingredient.

Life is just like that. The trials that we go through serve as the bitter, unsweetened chocolate. Life can serve up some pretty awful things, but the truth is that our maturity and character would be lacking if we never went through any difficulties. The Lord not only allows them, but He is able to use these elements to work His divine grace into us and give us greater confidence in the face of difficulties.

James 1:2-4, Count it all joy when you encounter various trials, knowing that the testing of your faith produces endurance. And let endurance have its perfect result, that you may be perfect and complete, lacking in nothing.

We must understand that James is not saying that somehow suffering is joyful. The joy is found in what the trial *produces* in us when we respond correctly. Did you notice what these trials are intended to produce?

Endurance. Endurance is the ability to continue on in the midst of difficulty. Endurance is the tenacity that says, "I won't quit no matter what happens." And that kind of endurance results in us being "perfect and complete, lacking nothing." Now that is a work of grace that's worth something -- even going through trials. This is the *joy* James is writing about.

What's strange is that too often after I come through a trial, I don't feel joy and I certainly don't feel perfect or complete. In fact, I am keenly aware of this lousy feeling that I still lack almost everything. So where did I go wrong? Did I fail the test? As a pastor friend once said, "The last thing I want to do is waste a good trial." So why don't I experience this feeling of perfection or completion and joy?

Perhaps some of the answer lies in Romans 5:1-5, where Paul shares a similar principle to the one in James when it comes to processing through a trial. Paul writes;

Therefore, having been justified by faith, we have peace with God through our Lord Jesus Christ, through whom also we have obtained our introduction by faith into this grace in which we stand; and we exult in hope of the glory of God. And not only this, but we also exult in our tribulations, knowing that tribulation brings about perseverance;

81

and perseverance, proven character; and proven character, hope; and hope does not disappoint because the love of God has been poured out within our hearts through the Holy Spirit who was given to us.

In the first couple of verses, Paul begins with a three-fold assurance of every believer. (vs. 1-2) He says:

1. We have been justified by faith.

2. We have access to the peace of God because of what Jesus has done.

3. We have hope or confidence to experience His glory.

This is all well and good until a trial or difficulty comes along.

During a trial, Satan loves to attack us when we're down. He brings three accusations that are in direct conflict with what Paul has described in these verses, the assurances that God desires us to experience as believers. In his assault, Satan whispers his lies, undermining God's very Word to us:

1. "The trial you're going through proves that you have no faith. After all, if you had real faith, you would not be in this trial."

2. "The trial proves that you are not at peace with God. If you were living rightly, God would protect you from the assault. Clearly, there must be sin in your life."

3. "The trial proves that you cannot be confident about walking in God's glory, and you probably never will be."

These lies serve two purposes. First to cast doubt on the finished work of Christ in our lives. Second, to keep us from experiencing the latter half of these verses which we will get to in a moment.

First let me say that our trials actually prove God's favor in our lives, not our failure. Remember, "whom the Lord *loves*, He disciplines" (Hebrews 12:6). I cannot think of one leader in the Old or New Testament who did not face trials and adversity and who did not come out the other side wiser, stronger, bolder, more confident, and more holy than before.

Satan will do all that he can to get our eyes off God's intentions for us through the trial. When we fall for his ploy, we tend to respond in the wrong way. It's a distraction. Instead of keeping our focus on God and

> ## Our trials actually prove God's favor in our lives

"counting it all joy" we end up with our focus on who is to blame for our circumstances, or trying to figure out what we did wrong.

During a trial, we must keep our focus on God's perspective and what He's trying to do in our lives, not the circumstances or people. In Psalm 23:5, David shares that "God prepares a table for us in the presence of our enemies." It's too easy for us to focus on our enemies rather than the amazing banquet that God has placed before us in the midst of it.

In the second half of Romans 5:3-5, Paul shares God's plans and intentions for us during the trial. When the stuff hits the fan, God wants to bring us into increasing levels of perseverance, proven character and a hope that does not disappoint because it leads us deeper into His love. It's knowing these truths that maximize our appreciation for the trial. The knowledge of these truths is why James says we can "rejoice when we encounter various trials," (James 1:2). God is taking us up a level.

Another way that we can fall into Satan's plans is to respond in anger. If we believe Satan's accusations and get our eyes off God's perspective, we will tend to follow our natural response. We can wrongly get angry at God, people or ourselves. Years after their trial, I still hear some pastors asking in anger; "Why did God allow this to happen?" They have become angry with God and still carry the pain of the trial. Others are still angry with the people who were involved, while others blame themselves.

Our wrong responses of anger are a continuation of Satan's plan for us to fail to come into all that God has for us through a trial. Please don't misunderstand me. I realize that a brief period of anger is natural. The Lord fully understands the agony in our hearts when we have been betrayed. To deny our pain could keep us from processing our wounds in a healthy way. What I am talking about is an anger that continues unabated for months or even years. Quite honestly, anger solves nothing and handled poorly produces nothing but bitterness.

A few verses after James tells us all the amazing benefits that a trial can produce, he says that the anger of man does not accomplish anything of God's purposes during a trial (James 1:20). Anger may be the natural response, but it is a waste of time and keeps us from the prize that God has set before us in the trial. The prize? Perseverance, proven character and a bigger heart filled with the love of God. The prize? Being made perfect, complete and lacking nothing. Almost makes you want to go through another trial, doesn't it? (I said almost).

CHAPTER FOUR

Wounded Wives

I (Steve) am eternally grateful for my wife, Michelle. She is a strong leader with a prophetic personality often seeing things as black and white. She is a wonderful teacher. At the same time, she has such a gracious, friendly way about her that people are just attracted her.

From the beginning of our time in ministry, we made it clear to every church that we were a team and that we co-pastored together. Of course, Michelle and I served in different roles in the church and I tried to allow her to do the things that she felt called to and that she was gifted in -- rather than allow the church to squeeze her into the traditional role of the pastor's wife; you know -- the person who plays piano, teaches Sunday School, and leads a ladies' prayer meeting.

For nearly 40 years of ministry (and 48 years of marriage), Michelle has stood by me or should I say that we stood together. For the most part, we have agreed on vision, ministry style, and church direction. She is in no way a wimpy woman so when I came under criticism, accusation, and attack, her standing by me was decisive, clear, and solid with full knowledge of all the issues. This is not to say that it didn't rip her guts out to have our family go through this, but it does mean that she stood with me in an amazing way. Her love and support were critical. Although we were both honest in seeing the weaknesses and mistakes in my life, Michelle was fully on my side. I felt fully supported and loved by the one person who knew me best and for that, I am eternally grateful. I don't know if I could have made it otherwise.

I am reminded of a young couple who pastored a few miles from us that we knew quite well. The wife was constantly approached by people in the church who criticized and complained to her about her husband. These were petty complaints and involved no issues of sin. She often felt torn in her heart and upset with her husband, siding with the fault finders. She came to us one day and asked why it was that no one came to Michelle to complain to her about me over petty issues. Michelle's answer was simple. "I wouldn't listen to it." It wasn't that people didn't try to complain, but she stopped them in their tracks, making it clear that she backed me and was fully supportive of me, despite my shortcomings and occasional lack of good judgment. There were occasions when

Michelle would bring up some of these topics with me privately and encourage me to strengthen some of these weak areas. But she never allowed herself to publicly side with anyone in opposition. This is to her credit. May I suggest that any wives reading this follow Michelle's example; it will save your husband and perhaps your marriage?

Something else that I would like to suggest to the ladies is that you help your husband *talk it out*. During times of accusation and attack, He will probably have no one else that he can really bear his heart to but you. But, before he will open his heart, he must know that you are on his side, even if he did blow it. He must know that you will not reject him, even if you are disappointed in him. If you are able to listen, reassure him, give honest/redemptive feedback and love him, it will allow him to process through this in a speedier, healthy way.

And finally, forgive the boldness, but may I also suggest that you bed him regularly during the crisis. When the stress and tension of these events attack your home and family, it can often result in a loss of sexual desire, especially for the women. However, there is a safe haven and a place of rest in the arms of a woman that no other place on this earth can provide for a man. Tenderly loving your husband in the midst of the crisis may provide healing like nothing else can. Part of this is because a man's worst fears are failure and rejection. By tenderly making love to him, you bring reassurance and acceptance to his heart.

Before Michelle shares her heart, how about some statistics about the ladies who stand by our sides in ministry and in the midst of crisis from Barna Research?

Pastors' Wives:

- 80% of pastors' wives feel their spouse is overworked.

- 80% of pastors' wives feel left out and unappreciated by the church members.

- 80% of pastors' wives wish their spouse would choose another profession.

- 80% of pastors' wives feel pressured to do things and be something in the church that they really are not.

My heart aches for the wives of those in church leadership who are in crisis because they carry a double burden. They carry the pain of their husband's accusation and rejection, and they carry their husbands and families on their heart while often suppressing their own needs, hurts, and emotions for the sake of the Kingdom. These are truly the honored ones.

Michelle's thoughts....

If you are the wife of a leader who has been wounded in ministry, you probably have some really deep wounds of your own, and often in the midst of the upheaval and the process of discipline and rejection, the wife gets overlooked or ignored. That is what happened to me. The leadership of our denomination gave little thought to what was happening in my own heart as they *dealt* with our situation and with my husband. It was as if what was happening to him didn't affect me at all. I even had one leader talk to me about "not taking up another's offense." Never mind that Steve and I were *one flesh*. I guess they didn't really believe that. I am thankful to one leader who pointed that out, and to a seasoned woman of God who observed, "A wife suffers *with* her husband, *for* her husband and *because* of her husband." That statement helped me gain some perspective on the situation, but the pain I experienced was still intense and very, very real.

> # A wife suffers *with* her husband *for* her husband and *because* of her husband

How do you navigate through the injustice, political machinery and religious nonsense taking place when you are hurting? I had no idea. Nothing prepares you for this type of test. You make mistakes. Attitudes you never knew you had, surface. You feel like scum. You experience shame, and rejection, and loneliness. You wonder how any godly believer, let alone a leader, could do what was done to you and your husband, and by extension, to your family and your church. You question everything you've believed and were taught. You question God. Everything is stripped away until only the core of who you are is left. You may even suffer an emotional breakdown. I did. I awoke one day and was unable to speak. I could barely move. I couldn't get dressed, couldn't eat; couldn't function. By God's grace, this was only temporary and was relieved through prayer. But for some, the breakdown continues for an extended period and they need a time of intense ministry in order to recover. My heart aches for them.

This Isn't What I Signed Up For

When Steve and I first met the Lord, it wasn't long before we knew that we would never be satisfied with anything less than full-time ministry. In both of us there was a deep desire to be sold-out to God and radically involved in His church. We jumped in with both feet, leading a young couple's group, teaching classes and attending any meetings where the Spirit was moving. Our local Christian businessmen's group provided both the opportunity to grow in the things of God as well as serve His people. It was at one of these meetings that Steve received a word that he would one day attend Bible school and enter the ministry, confirming what was already in our hearts. We put that word on the back burner and waited for the Lord's timing, thinking it would be many years before that happened. Little did we know that within two years God would speak again and we would move across the state and begin our training.

What an adventure we are on, I thought. I was excited that we were on our way. I wanted to learn and experience all of God that I could and partner with my husband in this high calling. I look back on that time as one of the happiest and most challenging but rewarding of our lives. Before graduation even arrived, we found ourselves called to serve a small-town congregation. Fruitful years followed as we saw people genuinely saved and brought into a fresh relationship with the Holy Spirit. Our small congregation grew.

There was fresh vision and excitement among the people, but in the background, trouble was brewing. Not everyone liked or agreed with what was happening in the church. Even as we were feeling the stirrings to move on to another place of service, we met and survived some skirmishes with those who opposed our leadership, and believing that our time of service there was ended, we resigned and returned to school to complete Steve's education.

Our next venture in ministry was pioneering a new church in a populated area of our state. I remember the Lord giving us the phrase "I am willing to spend and be spent for you," and we went in with that attitude. Again, we experienced growth and were able to plant a church in this new area, obtaining a building and growing over the years to 200+ attendees. We wanted more than anything else to lead a group of people into a deeper relationship with Jesus, without the religion, politics, and nonsense that seemed to characterize so much of the American church in those days.

I was stunned when the district overseer of our denomination met with Steve and me to tell us that he had received serious accusations against Steve and an investigation was being launched to determine the truth. This isn't what I had signed up for. We were told to just go on pastoring our church fellowship while this investigation went forward and to not mention anything. How does anyone do that? How do you smile and pretend that everything is fine, all the while knowing your life and ministry are on the line and that people you have loved and served (you don't know who) may be tearing you apart behind your back?

Muddling Through

I remember the day we met with leaders to hear the results of the three-month investigation. I had spent much time in prayer during those months, crying out to God for peace and for the truth to win the day. I had had many long and detailed talks with Steve about what he was accused of. "Was any of it accurate? Have you hidden things from me through the years? Why is this happening?" The strange thing was that we *really did* lead together. Steve rarely ministered apart from me. Even when he met for counseling, I was there or at least present in the next room. I was with him almost constantly. So much of what was being said was totally absurd, *yet our denominational leaders entertained it,* seemingly at the drop of a hat. I felt like the bottom had dropped out from under me, that there was no solid ground anymore in our ministry or our marriage and I couldn't tell what was real or what wasn't. So, when they arrived at our house to give us their findings, to put it mildly, I was very much on edge.

94

The Findings

To put it succinctly, we were told that they could substantiate none of the more serious accusations after having spoken with everyone making them, except for something vaguely called "coarse jesting." But even so – they were asking Steve to *step down from ministry* since the investigation itself had stirred up turmoil in the church and they felt a time away would be good for both us and the church. An interim pastor would take over the day-to-day affairs of the fellowship for a period of three months after which time we could return to lead again. They also stipulated that Steve was to see a clinical psychologist to make sure he was emotionally balanced. At one point when Steve was out of the room, I asked them to give me an example of something Steve had said that warranted such a decision and was told that once in a confrontation with our ex-son-in-law Steve had said that he was "pissed off" every time he saw our daughter write a check to cover the $40,000 in debts her ex-husband had racked up. *THAT WAS IT?* It just didn't add up.

(It was interesting to us that they only spoke with those who had a supposed grievance -- but not with anyone else. Our church secretary for instance, who worked closely with Steve for years, was never contacted, nor were others we were close to in the church. It just seemed like a lopsided way to conduct an inquiry.)

Facing The Shame

So POW! Just like that, we were no longer to pastor the church we had founded years before. In order to fulfill our commitment to be submitted to those in authority over us, we obeyed, even though we found it difficult to agree with their decision. For me, sitting on the front row the evening Steve announced his "stepping-down" from the church was emotional overload. I felt embarrassment and shame. I was angry, confused and deeply, deeply hurt. I felt like I was caught in a killer tornado, spinning out of control and fearful of …. well…. just fearful. My trust in God, in leaders and everyone else, was shaken that night. I could make sense of none of what had happened, of none of what our leaders had decided or of events I had personally lived through but that were being twisted by others. In the days that followed I remember the *push,* it took just for me to go grocery shopping and the anxiety about running into someone I knew. *What would they think? Would they even acknowledge me? Would I know how to act?* Not one pastor or church leader from our community contacted us during those months afterward. We really did go through it on our own and so for me, struggling with loneliness and having no one to help me process things was very difficult.

What About The Overseers?

This was another big question for me. *What about the men and women I had loved, honored and submitted to for years?* How was I to process their behavior and apparently unjust methods and decisions? After all, *these were our leaders!* How could they be wrong? But if they were right . . . where did that leave Steve . . . and me? My confidence on every level went out the window, and I struggled for years trying to put the crisis in perspective and move on.

Letting Go

Perhaps some wives navigate such storms much better than I did. Perhaps they're better at processing events and settling issues, but for me, the struggle continued at the deepest levels of my being for a long, long time. I lived for years pretty much dead inside, always hoping that the next church or ministry venture would rekindle life in my heart once again. I felt as if I was "watching myself live" – not actually living. I also spent years reviewing the details of the situation in my mind trying to make sense of it all. Although I had all the facts of the situation, it never made sense to me. Thankfully, the Lord in His goodness has

97

made a way for my heart to heal and I've learned many valuable lessons along the way.

I want to share briefly some thoughts on what God was doing in me as the wife of an accused leader.

There are traps along the way when you travel any difficult road, like the traps along the road in *The Pilgrim's Progress,* the classic story by John Bunyon. I wish I could report that I escaped them all, but I can't. But even if you fall into a trap or two, (or three or four) God is at work on the inside in ways you often don't recognize at the time.

The first trap I fell into was overanalyzing the situation. I replayed every detail from start to finish over and over again. I could not shut my thinking off about the situation. I became fixated – trying desperately to understand – to make sense of what had happened. Part of this was just because of who I am in my own person. I had always been a good student, winning scholarships and excelling in almost every subject. What that did was build an almost unshakeable confidence in my own ability to reason things out. But here I was faced with a situation that made no sense. Try as I might – nothing added up. The outcome of this pattern was the shutting down of my heart, and that in turn affected my ability to have confidence in God.

It all had to do with trust. Because I had once trusted the leadership who entertained the accusations, it somehow affected my ability to trust God. I also doubted that what I was hearing from Him was accurate. On top of that, I discovered that replaying the events over and over in my mind was really a control issue. I was trying to take control of the events and the outcome – as if by sorting it all out I could change the future. The Word tells us to "take every thought captive" not to replay every thought over and over. I had to let go and learn to trust the Lord and not rely on my own ability to accurately understand. Now, some 20 years later, I am still learning to let go and recognize that there are some things in life that will remain in the realm of the unknown. Finding the grace to let the unknown go and live at peace with the mystery of it all is bringing life back to my heart. After all – only God has 360-degree vision. The adage really is true that you can't start the next chapter of your life if you keep re-reading the last one. Lesson learned.

Another trap I experienced is the trap of *false beliefs*. A trauma of this nature reveals any cracks in the foundation of your belief system. Most of us live our lives secure in what we believe, but what if what we believe is faulty? One such belief for me was the notion that if we lived life according to the will of God as revealed in His Word, we would be kept from serious trials. And like many false beliefs, you don't know they're there until something brings them to light. I would have argued intensely that I understood the fallacy of such a belief, but the truth was that even though on the surface I agreed such a thing was untrue, deep down I really believed it.

A second false belief I inadvertently carried inside was the idea that the Lord had loved us so much that He had placed us in an extraordinary denomination, one where I could rest my heart without fear. Was that idea ever blown apart! What had really happened was that I had idealized and idolized our leaders, could never imagine being a part of any other group and didn't want to be. I'm sure you can recognize this for what it is – idolatry – and being a jealous God, the Lord could not let that go unaddressed. We are admonished in the Word not to put our hope or trust in man – who will surely fail us – but sometimes you must live a thing for it to become real in you. No man, no leader, no denomination can ever take God's rightful place in us.

The next issue I found myself dealing with was one of identity. I loved being a pastor's wife. I loved leading a group of believers, loved growing in my gifts and calling, loved carrying a vision for establishing a kingdom church in the valley in which we lived. I felt God's hand on my life –

felt His call into greater ministry. I loved that Steve released and encouraged me to follow the Spirit's leading in my life – and suddenly – it was all gone! Now what?

And so, the question became, who am I really? Who am I in God? It's at this point that who the scriptures said I was in Christ had to become flesh in me, not just Bible verses or Christian clichés. I spent months in the Psalms, identifying with all the raw emotions they contained, but also receiving at much deeper levels the truths of who I was as God's child. Spending that time in this wonderful book was a life-saver. It allowed me to connect the new creation truths of the New Testament with the humanity of a follower of God portrayed in the Old.

One last issue I faced was the issue of prayer. I believe in prayer. It's part of the spiritual DNA I received when I was born again. Prayer was my lifeline to God. I connected to His heart regularly and easily through the years, so when we first faced this trial, I turned to the Lord in prayer with fasting. I believed prayer changes things, that God hears and answers and that as the God of justice, He would vindicate my husband and our ministry. BUT HE DIDN'T! For me, the question then became, *Why not? Hadn't I prayed enough? Had I prayed wrongly? Wasn't my fast good enough? Was it too short? Were my efforts too weak? Why didn't my prayers work?* For a long time I beat myself up, believing that I had let my husband down because if I had been praying rightly, things would have turned out differently. It took me quite a while to work through this point, to understand, really understand deep inside that I couldn't use prayer to control situations, that God is in charge and will direct our lives according to His wisdom, not ours.

In His grace, the Lord has been teaching me to trust Him once again. Perhaps what I've realized is that my trust in Him was based too much on outward circumstances. When things were going good, I could trust Him. When things were going bad, my trust was shaken. Through this crisis, I am coming to know that "Though He slay me, I will hope in Him," (Job 13:15). Realizing that His leadership is perfect and that He always has my best interest in mind, I can rest fully in Him.

Lingering Pain and Sorrow.

I still experience pain and sorrow from time to time over what we went through. In some ways, it has been like experiencing the death of a loved one. There is grief over the losses -- friendships, ministry relationships, home, etc. I mourned the losses for quite a while, and in some ways, still do, but I learned to live with it. For me, the most difficult thing to live with is watching two of my children live far away from the Lord as a direct result of what we endured. My mother's heart is continually broken and burdened for them, crying out to God for their healing and restoration. At times it is difficult to remain unoffended toward those who precipitated this trial because of where our daughters are in their hearts. I must continually cry out to God for His grace to believe that He is working behind the scenes to restore them to Himself

In the end, there is nowhere else to turn but to the Lord. Even during times when you are angry with Him for allowing the trial, you know you have no other hope outside of Him. It takes time, but as the days and weeks unfold and your heart begins to heal, relationship with Him begins to be restored and peace begins to enfold you once again. It may start only as a trickle, but it is real, and under His wings, you will again find refuge.

We're Not Alone In This

The effects of this kind of crisis impact most families of clergy. Dennis Maynard found that most of these clergy (who went through a church crises) reported that their spouses and one or more of their children will no longer attend a church of any kind. This was further compounded by our clergy participants themselves who reported that their participation in church life is now rare to never.

CHAPTER FIVE

Coming Back What A Mess We're In

There is a great percentage of pastors who never seem to find their way back after going through a major crisis in the church. After 20 years of researching pastoral trends distilled from *Barna, Focus on the Family,* and *Fuller Seminary,* as well as talking to lots of wounded pastors, we have found that pastors are in a dangerous occupation! We are perhaps in the single most stressful and frustrating working profession, more than medical doctors, lawyers, politicians or cat groomers (hey cats have claws). Just last week I was at Applebee's having dinner with a brother that I've known for nearly 40 years. He had pastored for quite some time but was now serving as an itinerant teacher, traveling most weekends both home and abroad to minister in churches. When I asked him "How are you really doing?" His reply was, "I'm not as stressed out as I was when I was pastoring. I'm much more at peace now." I didn't expect that answer for two reasons. First, he never seemed to be a stressed out individual. And secondly, when I think about the hassles of leaving home most every Thursday, catching a flight somewhere, dealing with the lines, delays, hotels, car rentals, meals with strangers, speaking, coming home on Mondays and doing it over and over again – I get stressed out just thinking about it.

Most research says that 60% to 80% of those who enter the ministry will not still be in ministry 10 years later, and only a fraction of all pastors will stay in ministry for a lifetime. Many pastors—I believe over 90 percent—start off with a true calling and the enthusiasm and the endurance of faith to make it, but something happens along the way to derail their train of passion and love for the calling into ministry.

Out of the 1050 pastors recently surveyed during two pastor's conferences held in Pasadena, California, 825, or 78% said they were forced to resign from a church *at least once*. Sixty-three percent said they had been fired from their pastoral position at least twice.

Over 70% of pastors stated the following five reasons for being forced from their church. Here are their responses in order:

Four hundred twelve (412 or 52%) stated that the number one reason for leaving their church was organizational and control issues. A conflict arose that forced them out based on who was going to lead and manage the church: pastor, elder, key lay person or faction.

1. One hundred ninety (190 or 24%) stated that the number one reason for leaving was their church was already in such a significant degree of conflict, the pastor's approach could not resolve it.

2. One hundred nineteen (119 or 14%) stated the number one reason was that the church was resistant to their leadership, vision, teaching, or to change; or that their leadership was too strong or too fast.

3. Sixty-four (64 or 8%) stated the number one reason to resign was that the church was not connecting with them on a personal level, or the church over-admired the previous pastor and would not accept them.

4. Forty (40 or 5%) stated that the number one reason that they were fired was not having the appropriate relational or connecting skills as a pastor. (It is interesting that no one mentioned lack of teaching ability— only that their teaching was not

accepted. Too many congregations want their ears tickled.

No wonder 70% of pastors fight depression. Their leadership is not valued, honored, or received. And not that pastors are in it for the money, but it does add insult to injury when most pastors are paid very poorly. I know when we started pastoring in 1978, our annual salary was just $10,000, even if it did include a parsonage, for a family of five, we often struggled.

"Lord, where can we go, You have the words of eternal life."

In John 6 many of Jesus' followers walked away from Him because He told them they would have to "eat the flesh of the Son of Man and drink His blood," (John 6:53). And I thought my sermon topics were a bit hard to swallow! The disciples stood there in shock. But rather than begging them to stay, Jesus simply asks, "You do not want to go away also, do you," (John 6:66-67)? The fact is, the hearers were scandalized. Repeatedly through the Gospels, Jesus says some hard statements to people, not for the purpose of being hard, but in order to test them and see if they would continue to believe and have faith in the midst of offense. It is one of the reasons that Jesus says, "Blessed is he who does not take offense at Me," (Matt. 11:6). Much of what Jesus did and said was misunderstood and offensive to His listeners.

Having been scandalized, you have the same choice to make concerning ministry and even concerning the Lord Himself. When you search your heart in response to following Christ or not, I would hope that you would come to the same conclusion that the 12 came to. Where can I go? There is only One who has the words of eternal life and only One worth laying our life down for in service. I'm reminded of the words of a song that says, "It's gonna be worth it, it's gonna be worth it, it's gonna be worth it all." This doesn't mean that you haven't got some anger or mistrust in your heart toward God, but I hope we will be able to help you process through those issues.

After going through the hellish events that so many pastors and Christian leaders have gone through, many pastors struggle with knowing how to come back. If there is a gulf between you and the Lord, how do you come back? If you are not currently involved in ministry but would like to be one day, how do you come back?

The Steps To Coming Back

Before you begin the steps to return to the Lord or serving Him, you should recognize that this is a process that may take a number of years -- not months -- years. To complicate the process, about the time that you think you are healthy and gaining ground, something will trigger an old memory and you'll find yourself in a tailspin, thinking some really bad thoughts toward God, toward others, and even yourself. Don't ask me how I know this. In that place, the first critical step that must be taken is that of forgiveness.

Forgiveness:

Let us look at several realities about Biblical forgiveness as this is one of the main keys to being set free from our wounds and is, in fact, the first step to restoration.

> **The only difference between the prisoners and the prison guards is which side of the bars you're on**

A good friend of mine, Dr. Fount Shults used to give a wonderful analogy about forgiveness. He said that when someone sins against you, you have every right to put him "in prison" (emotionally) until they have paid their debt to you. It is a prison not made with hands, but it is a prison built in our own hearts. However, as with all prisons, the prisoners must be guarded to make sure they don't *escape* before they've paid their debt in full. We are assigned the task of being the prison guards. We are assigned to continually keep them in the prison of our hearts, making sure that they remain locked up for what they did. We do this by constantly remembering the hurt they caused and refusing to forgive their offense. Unfortunately, as with all prisons, it is confining, depressing and hard. The only difference between those locked inside the prison and the guards who keep them in there is which side of the bars they're on. As guardians of the offense, making sure that they never get out, we also end up living our lives in that dark, gloomy place of unforgiveness. The result is that we don't get out either. Genuine forgiveness from the heart is the only thing that will set the prisoner (and us) free from that awful place.

A Choice Not A Feeling

I remember not long after we were wounded, we realized that we were not going to progress in God unless we found the way to forgive our enemies. This was difficult because we had just finished building our dream house down the street from the church that we had been thrown out of. We began building there because things were great in the church and we thought that we would live there and even retire from that church. It was just before moving in that all Hell broke loose. Now, we lived there and each day I would have to drive past *their* facility on our way into town. I had all I could do to not make foul gestures or do a drive-by mooning. Oh, the maturity!

Over the years I have heard many Christians say that "forgiveness is a choice, not a feeling." I both agree and disagree. After being deeply wounded, I realize that forgiveness usually *starts* as a choice because there is no way that our emotions are going to respond in a godly manner. At this point in time, we must obey God's commands to forgive our enemies, but it will be a matter of choice, not emotion. During this process, you can feel a little schizophrenic because you are choosing one thing but feeling another. This may be the current reality, but we cannot stay there.

In time, forgiveness *must* begin to move to the realm of feeling or emotion. It must touch the very core of our emotions. To say that we have forgiven without our emotions being engaged is to fall short of true forgiveness. In Matthew 18:22, where Jesus speaks of forgiving our enemies seventy times seven, He goes on to say that if we do not forgive "from the heart" we are not forgiven from the Father. This, of course, is a process. The fact that Jesus uses multiplication indicates a process. But the process of choosing to forgive someone over and over again eventually leads to the complete forgiveness which includes our emotions. The anger is gone, the hostility is gone, the poison is out of our system and they no longer have a debt owed to us: we've released them. Whether they still may owe a debt before God is yet to be known.

When Michelle and I began to make the choice to forgive, it was exactly that -- a choice. We would grit our teeth and say things like "God, I forgive those rotten so and so's." It doesn't get more spiritual than that! Several times a day, as painful feelings and memories came to the surface, we were given the choice to forgive or harden our hearts in unforgiveness, keeping our prisoners locked up. So, each day we dutifully chose to forgive. As time went on, we began to discover something. We found that our prayers of forgiveness had less and less venom in them. In time it actually became easier to forgive and actually feel it. At one point, in an attempt to bless our enemies, Michelle decided to make a large, two-sided banner for their new sanctuary. This was a labor of love that took her months. The banner was presented and to our knowledge they still have it. We had made the choice to forgive and bless our enemies but now our positive emotions were beginning to get involved. It took some time, but we were finally able to bless our enemies as a choice coupled with genuine feelings of forgiveness.

Just as a side note, five years after our ordeal we were able to sit down and be fully reconciled with that church and its pastor. Since then, I have had the joy of speaking in a couple of Sunday services there. Furthermore, we were eventually re-credentialed with the denomination involved until we moved out of the area. I am not sure we have heard of more than a few reconciliations to such a degree.

Saying The Words

One of the real traps that we have discovered is that Christians tend to shy away from actually saying the words "I forgive you." As a pastor, I have had the joy of sitting many times with two parties trying to see their relationship healed and reconciled. After some time - and occasionally some coaxing - one person will finally say; "Please forgive me." Too often the other person will respond by saying; "Oh, it's okay" rather than specifically saying, "I forgive you." But the words are important. I'm not sure how, but something happens spiritually and emotionally as we say and hear those words when they come from the heart.

The Steps Of Forgiveness

Having sighted some of the pitfalls and misunderstandings of forgiveness, what does the process look like? May we walk you through it step by step? Perhaps this seems beneath you as a church leader, but the truth is that in your pain you may not be fully functioning in all that you know from the Word.

Now that you have chosen to forgive and follow that process until your emotions are engaged in a healthy way, let's look at what steps you should take to forgive someone. During our time in Kansas City, I had the joy of team teaching a class on inner healing with our good friend, Mary Leonard. She showed us these five practical steps to forgiveness that you need to consider. They are:

1. Take an account
2. Accept the loss
3. Exchange the pain
4. Cancel the debt
5. Speak a blessing

Take An Account:

After someone has been wounded they usually spend far too much time licking their wounds. That is, they replay the event over and over in their minds, as Michelle shared, usually resulting in either condemning or justifying themselves. This almost always refuels their anger. Taking an account is neither.

To take an account of the situation with the goal of forgiveness means that you sit down and think through (perhaps even write) everything that this hurtful event cost you. The emphasis is on your pain -- not their sin. For example: When we were taking an account of our situation, we realized that we lost our reputation, the church that we had pioneered, our relationships with other leaders, and our only means of income at the time. But it didn't end there. It also affected our girls, who were then young adults. They were deeply wounded by the church and as a result haven't been back to church in any meaningful way since. There was a tremendous cost.

> # When we forgive, we should know exactly what we're forgiving

When we forgive, we should know exactly what we're forgiving. When we go to the Lord asking for forgiveness, does He not ask us to confess our sins specifically? Perhaps you feel that "taking an account" is forbidden by Paul's admonition of love which "keeps no record of wrongs," (1 Cor. 13:5). Keeping a record of wrongs is just the opposite of taking an account in order to forgive. We're not to keep a record or list of offenses to remind us of all the dirt that was done to us so that we can go on justifying our anger, but we can take stock of our losses to recognize what the situation cost us. Remember Matt. 18:23? Jesus tells the story of a king who wanted to "settle accounts" with his servants. He knew exactly what each man owed him. Too often Christians have taken no specific account of the wounds that they have suffered during an offense. Until an accurate account has been taken, your forgiveness will be based on only that which is currently in your memory.

At the same time, when someone comes and says, "Please forgive me," I am not suggesting that you make them wallow in their guilt by pulling out a scroll with all their offenses listed. I am not suggesting that you make them confess every offense specifically. What I am saying is that in order to forgive fully, *you* need to know what you are forgiving, period.

Accept The Loss:

Someone once said that history can be redeemed but it cannot be changed. This means that you have got to grapple with the fact that what you have lost in the process of the crisis, is lost. Outside of God's restoration power, whatever form that takes, you will not get back what you lost. Accept it, let it go and get over it. It is done. Hanging onto it only deepens the wound. It may have cost you your position, your income, or your reputation.

You must be able to accept the losses by laying them at the feet of Jesus and letting them go. The Lord in His mercy often restores these things to us, many times in greater measure than we had at the beginning. But until He does, they are gone.

Exchange The Pain:

Having counted the cost of what you have lost and been willing to accept that it is gone and knowing that you will probably not get it back, you are now at the place of your deepest pain. This is the hardest place to be in during the process. Now you are able to go to the Lord and pour it out on Him. You are able to cry through all that you have lost and the pain of it. Now you are at the place where you can give it all to Him. Exchange your pain for His comfort. Give Jesus your sorrow and let Him begin to give you His peace. Allow Him to wipe away your tears. The truth of exchanging your pain for His peace is His promise to you and you can begin the process immediately. Recognize that it will probably be a process of exchange that may take months and sometimes years, but with each tear you give Him, He will release deeper peace in your heart. Psalm 56:8 tells us that we can ask God to put our tears in His bottle, confident that He knows our journey of pain and our desire to press forward in forgiveness.

Cancel The Debt:

As you go through this process, there will come a point (hopefully sooner than later) that you will be able to cancel the debt owed to you. We need to understand that forgiveness is the gift of giving a pardon instead of requiring full payment. This is what has happened to us when we accepted Christ. When we asked Him to forgive us our sins (debts), it was real debt and a real payment needed to be made. "We have not been redeemed by perishable things like silver and gold, but by the precious blood of Christ," (1 Peter 1:18). By choosing to forgive your enemies you have recognized that there was a genuine debt. You have taken an account, exchanged the pain of it for God's mercy and peace and you are able to release the person of the obligation of payment. That is forgiveness! Still, we're not quite through.

Speak a Blessing:

This is only truly possible when the first four steps have been completed. When you are able to bless your enemies and mean it, you have gained freedom. This took me several years. As I said earlier, I could say the words of forgiveness, but they had not yet penetrated the emotional levels of anger. Once I walked through all the steps of forgiveness, only then was I able to speak a blessing and mean it.

Be aware that forgiveness, reconciliation, and trust are three entirely different issues. Forgiveness is the first step in the process and is *entirely your responsibility*. The Lord has already told us to forgive our enemies, now it's up to us to do it. You do not even need to have the other party present to forgive. This is between you and God and He will give you the grace to forgive. Forgiveness is a requirement of the Lord and not optional. Matt. 6:12, 15.

Reconciliation happens when both parties come together with a heart of humility, willing to take responsibility for their own actions and the other's pain. Both parties may feel that they are in the right, but this must be laid down for the higher principles of the Word. There are times when someone is wounded, and the other party is not even aware of it. This happens all the time between a husband and wife. She is hurt, and he has no clue why. Reconciliation will not happen until they are both willing to forgive and he is willing to ask forgiveness, even when he did not intentionally wound her.

Trust, however, is another issue altogether. All believers are called to love. All believers are called to be reconciled to their brothers. In fact, we've been given the "ministry of reconciliation," (2 Cor. 5:18). Trust, however, is different and separate from love and reconciliation. This only makes sense. We may be commanded to "love our enemies," (Matt. 5:44), but it would be absurd to trust them. Of course, in a healthy relationship, trust is a real bonus. I like to say it this way. We are commanded to love but trust is a gift. There is nothing automatic about it. It may take years to build trust. Trust is a delicate commodity that is fragile in nature. Someone has said, trust takes years to build, seconds to break, and forever to repair. Honestly, in church disputes, it is rare to see genuine forgiveness take place between parties. It is extremely rare to see reconciliation. And it borders on the miraculous to see trust reestablished. I'd say it is impossible, but with God.... May the Lord take us to a higher level of His heart in dealing with dissension in the church.

Now that we understand the differences between forgiveness, reconciliation, and trust, we better understand that speaking a blessing flows from the command to love. It is a part of love, an extension of God's grace and goodness, even to those who do not deserve it. It is the ability to bless and pray God's best for people. It does not require reconciliation or rebuilt trust. As we have completed the last step of forgiveness and find the grace to speak a blessing, even over our enemies, I believe that we experience a deep level of God's blessing in return.

Ungodly Beliefs

If you have been through a crisis in your church or denomination it is almost impossible to come away without lasting wounds. I remember saying that I wish there was a book on how to walk through a church crisis when we were going through ours. How do you keep your heart right? How do you keep from reacting or defending yourself? Should you stay and defend yourself or just walk away? And how do you protect your heart from getting smashed again?

As a natural defense, we often end up believing lies that we feel are true. We call these *ungodly beliefs*. These beliefs can be about ourselves, others, the church or even God. Let me give you a personal example. Years after our crisis, through ministry from some friends, I came to realize that I had developed a whole set of beliefs that really weren't true, even though they felt true. They included things like; "You really can't trust lay leadership, they will eventually turn on you." Another was "I am too unconventional for the pastorate; therefore, I will be rejected again." These beliefs were formed in my thinking as a result of the pain I went through. Some other ungodly beliefs I've heard over the years are, "Don't do business with Christians, they will eventually cheat you." "You can't trust church leaders." and the ever popular, "Everyone in the church is a hypocrite."

As I relate to wounded leaders I find that most of them have believed several lies about church ministry and people. In addition, as we struggle with our pain we may even believe that God can't be trusted because He stood by and allowed us to go through the crisis. I'll share my personal struggle with this in the pages ahead.

The hardest thing about dealing with ungodly beliefs is that they seem so true. Combating them often feels like we are going against the truth. Every fiber of our being can resist this process. However, the only way to navigate through the lies is to come back to the foundation of God's Word, regardless of our feelings or experience.

The first step in dealing with ungodly beliefs is to identify the lies. Because of the nature of these lies, they are often best discovered with the help of another trusted friend or counselor. In the appendix, we have also included an Ungodly Beliefs Discovery Sheet that will help you discover yours. As you fill out the sheet please be aware that *all* the items listed *are* in fact, ungodly beliefs -- that is, they are lies and contrary to the Truth.

Once you have discovered your ungodly beliefs, the next step is to repent for believing them. Remember, they are lies. They are contrary to God's truth. Therefore, it is an affront to God to have believed that which is contrary to Him and His nature. You must break agreement with them. This means that it is not enough to just recognize them and repent of them, but you need to actually say; "I no longer agree with the lie that _____."

Finally, I suggest that you write out God's corresponding truth to *each* of your ungodly beliefs. For example, if you have believed the lie that says; "God will not use me because I am nothing but a failure," the corresponding truth might be, "For the gifts and the calling of God are irrevocable," (Rom. 11:29). We can also take courage from the many leaders throughout the Scriptures that God used, despite their evident failures. I love reading about the life of David but let's be honest, he made lots of mistakes and often failed God. Yet, when his life is recounted in the book of Acts, it says of David that he was "A man after My heart, who will do all my will" and "After he had served the purposes of God in his own generation..." (Acts 13:22, 36). You may *feel* like a failure, but I wonder how God will recount your life?

It is important to allow the Holy Spirit to guide you through this process. Michelle and I were encouraged to write out our ungodly beliefs and the corresponding truths with a compatible scripture and then read/pray through the truths every day for a month until we began to really believe these new truths. As we've ministered these truths to others, we've been amazed to see their countenance change as the weight of these lies were lifted off and replaced with God's truth. Again, feel free to use the Ungodly Belief Discovery Sheet in the appendix.

Ungodly beliefs almost always lead to inner vows.

Inner Vows

An inner vow is a promise that you make in your heart which is basically designed to protect you from the pain of the lie that you have believed. These vows may be a clear conscious decision, or they may exist at the subconscious level. A simple example of an inner vow and how the process of healing might work is as follows: Let's say that I have been wounded in an ugly divorce. Out of the pain of that event, I form a belief (which is really an ungodly lie) that *all women* will take advantage of you if you give them the chance. I then make an inner vow that I will never trust a woman again.

Do you see how my ungodly belief fueled my inner vow about women? This ungodly belief may be expressed every time I open my mouth. I may say statements like; "I can tell you one thing, you can't trust a woman." Or they may become buried in our subconscious and not even be active in our thinking. But, they may still have an effect on my decisions. Perhaps, years later, I meet a woman and decide to pursue a deeper relationship. I may be struggling in my new relationship to be open, transparent and honest because of the power of these lies working subconsciously in my heart. As the relationship progresses, she becomes more and more frustrated because I won't open up and I in turn ultimately sabotage the relationship by remaining closed.

These inner vows must be recognized, repented of, broken and resisted in order to be set free of their power.

The Conclusion of My Personal Story

I Thought You Had My Back

In October of 2016, some 25 years since our church crises, I went on a men's retreat with the church we were attending. *I love men's retreats,* I thought to myself. *Volleyball, some hiking, sharing around a campfire, some good chapel times. This will be great.* When I arrived, I found that there were only about 15 men. *This will still work,* I thought.

As the retreat leaders led us into the discussion on the first night of the weekend, I realized that this was going to be a different type of retreat than any I had ever been on. No volleyball, no games, nothing like that. It was going to be an intense time of dealing with issues, hurts, rejections, fears, and sin in our hearts: a spiritual boot camp! *Oh great, just my cup of tea.*

Aside from the leaders, I was the only one there who had pastored before, so I mentally put myself into the uninvited position of *support minister* to those *poor hurting brothers.* As the retreat unfolded I began to feel more and more as though God wanted to heal something in my heart that I wasn't sure I had even identified yet.

It began the second day when they showed a short clip from the movie *The Bear.* I had seen this cute nature movie depicting a grizzly cub whose mother is killed, leaving him to fend for himself in the Canadian Rockies. It becomes clear that this cub hasn't got a chance against the many predators, especially a mountain lion that has been hunting him for a few days. The inevitable happens when the lion corners the bear cub at a raging river. With nowhere to run, the cub instinctively rises up on his back two legs and begins growling at the lion with his almost childlike voice. The camera does a great job showing the huge cougar cowering back and retreating! As the cameral slowly broadens its scope, we see that there is a huge adult grizzly just behind the cub, also standing on his back legs growling at the lion. No wonder the lion backs off!

The leader stopped the clip at that point and said to us, "Others may fail you in a crisis, but God always has your back." With that statement, everything inside me broke. Completely undone, I realized that I did not trust the Lord because I felt that when my enemies came to destroy me, God didn't have my back. He let me experience failure, rejection, loneliness, abandonment, pain and loss. I sat there, in front of everyone, crying uncontrollably.

As I shared with the retreat leaders what I was going through they began to focus on my pain and ask God the best way to minister to this deep hurt. I realized that I just didn't understand why the Lord had allowed such a thing to happen. I took a few moments to share the synopsis of the crisis I had gone through years before in the church. Suddenly one of the senior pastors that I respected, pulled a chair up right in front of me and said; "I'm going to sit here before you and role play any of those involved in the situation so that you can ask *any* question that you want."

At this point in time, I had pretty much processed through all the rejection and accusation from the people involved so many years before. The only one left in my mind was the Lord. So, I took a deep breath and said; "I have processed through almost all the pain inflicted by people. The one I don't understand is you, God. Why did you let me go through all of that? Why didn't you stop my enemies from their vicious attacks and vindicate me? Why didn't you have my back?" As I asked these pointed questions, I wasn't feeling any anger. I just didn't understand, and I was deeply hurt.

After a few moments of silence, the leader sitting in front of me finally responded as from the Lord. As best as I can remember (as I was a total wreck emotionally) he said, "I am so sorry my son for the pain and all that you went through. But you must know that I was with you through it all. I never did abandon you or leave you, not for a moment. I let you go through what you did because I counted you worthy to experience that which my own Son experienced. I counted you worthy to suffer the pain, rejection, and loss that He did so that you might strengthen others. For indeed 'you are My beloved son in whom I am well pleased.'"

I thought I was weeping before! Without realizing it, that leader had spoken the very words prophesied over me at my ordination! I suddenly realized that it was His great love that allowed me the honor of going through what I did, allowing me to share in the sufferings of Christ. A chain inside snapped and broke, and I felt as though the healing of my heart was now complete.

This account is an example of a powerful time of healing for me, a necessary part of my own journey. I pray that the words of my testimony will somehow reach through your pain and touch your heart. I don't know the circumstances of your pain or the hurts that you've been through. But I do know that the Lord loves you and has always had your back. He's always had your best in mind. He's always been on your side.

CHAPTER SIX

I'm Not Sure I Wanted To Hear That

I Beg Your Pardon, I Never Promised You A Rose Garden

I often reflect on the words that Job uttered after the enemy had sifted him like wheat. Job 13:15 says, "Though He slay me, yet will I trust Him..." ("will hope in Him" in some translations). Now I'm not sure that God kills our ministries, He probably just stands back and watches them die, but the outcome is the same --"They dead!" And the pain and loss accompanying that death, no matter how it happens, is very real. We shouldn't be shocked. After all, Jesus said that we must take up our cross and follow Him, (Matt. 16:24). The reality is that there is a death sentence on our lives. Jesus also said that "unless a grain of wheat falls into the ground and dies, it abides alone," (John 12:24). And Paul said that he "died daily" in his service to Christ, (1 Cor. 15:31)

Before I went into the ministry, I remember crying out many times for the Lord to *use me*. Then when He did, I was shocked that I felt *used*. What did we expect -- really? If I'm not mistaken, every one of the 12 Apostles was martyred -- except John who was boiled in oil, didn't die, but then was banished to an island prison. (Which I'm not sure was a better deal.) It is in this very process where we "share in the sufferings of Christ," (1 Pet. 4:13). And if you have suffered loss in ministry, count yourself among the greats.

Understand that death (however it comes and whatever form it takes) comes to *all* believers, not just leaders. Therefore, in my mind, the focus cannot be about the wounds that I suffered through the process of dying, rather, it's my response to the process of dying that is critical. Job said, "Yet will I trust Him," (Job 13:15). Wow! This is clearly a *choice* that he made and that we also must make as we process through the pain of death. To not embrace the process is to only delay coming to peace. But how can we make the choice to trust the Lord when it seems like all hope is lost?

Trashed Dreams In My Heart

While grappling to come to peace with the idea that we are going through a dying process -- and ultimately at the permissive hands of God, we will have to let go of some of our dreams. As a young pastor, I had so many grand dreams of what ministry and my life would look like. I saw myself impacting large crowds of people. I thought that I would travel and touch the nations. I believed that our ministry would impact thousands. I'm certain that some of these dreams were birthed in the zeal of an immature heart, but they were none the less real. After a crisis, our dreams lay on the floor in a heap, smashed to pieces. And like Humpty Dumpty, neither the King's horses nor the King's men can put them back together again. Yes, the death is real. I have a thought that might bring healing to your heart in this, but first, let me also mention the unfulfilled promises of God.

Unfulfilled Promises From God

If it wasn't hard enough to have to bury my personal dreams for ministry, I realized that there were several promises for ministry that God has whispered to my heart over the years that have also died and now must be buried. This is sacred stuff. Many of these promises came during profound encounters with God. I can recall the time, date, place and circumstances of these promises vividly. Many of them I still carry in my heart, having never shared them with anyone but my wife. These were promises that kept us going in the early days of ministry when we were discouraged. Many of the promises were so profound and majestic in scope that we often wondered how they could even happen, but God.

For many of you reading these words, there seems to be no way God's promises can come to pass, outside of a miraculous resurrection. In addition, how do we reconcile the confident belief that these were *God's promises* that we're talking about with their apparent death? If my dreams die that's one thing, but how can God's promises go unfulfilled? After all, as I mentioned earlier, aren't His gifts and calling without repentance? How is it even possible that the actions of men (especially some of the men involved in my situation) could thwart the plans of God?

Are we supposed to just keep on believing? The answer is, perhaps so. There are plenty of examples in the scripture where the sages of old "had to hope against all hope," (Rom. 4:18). The first half of Hebrews 11 gives us example after example of those who had faith and ultimately saw the fulfillment of the promise. Heb. 11:33-34 sums up their accomplishments, saying, "who by faith conquered kingdoms, performed acts of righteousness, obtained promises, shut the mouths of lions, quenched the power of fire, escaped the edge of the sword, from weakness were made strong, become mighty in war, and put foreign armies to flight." They had faith and saw the promises fulfilled.

However, just a few verses later, (vs 39) the writer honors those who "gained approval through their faith but *had not* received <u>what was promised</u>...." We must read and consider what the scripture says of these saints. Their stand in faith was genuine and must be honored regardless of the outcome. These are such powerful verses that I want to suggest that you read them a few times; even as you reflect on the promises you have believed in faith even though they've not been fulfilled.

Others were tortured, not accepting their release, in order that they might obtain a better resurrection; and others experienced mocking and scourging, yes, also chains and imprisonment. They were stoned, they were sawn in two, they were tempted, they were put to death with the sword, they went about in sheepskins, in goatskins, being destitute, afflicted, ill-treated (men of whom the world was not worthy), wandering in deserts and mountains and caves and holes in the ground...did not receive what was promised. Heb. 11:35 - 39

You see, what is promised may be our focus, but our ability to have faith, regardless, is God's. It's a test with significant weight to it.

Who Are We Trusting In?

I don't believe that the choice to trust God is an empty choice, a choice made just for the Hell of it or a choice based on sheer stupidity. I believe that it is a choice based on substance, on solid Biblical truth, on a hope that is "anchored....within the veil," (Heb. 6:19), on the promises of God which are sure and steadfast and immovable. We are trusting in nothing less than the character of God, and He never lies. Promises that are genuinely from God are always "yes and amen" in Christ and they *will come to pass*. Why? Because "He who promised is faithful," (Heb. 10:23).

The challenge that we face in a crisis is that often our "truster" gets broken. After we went through our crisis, I had trouble trusting the church, trusting leaders, trusting what I had believed, and sadly, trusting God. This was partly due to the fact that somehow, I bought into the current trendy theology that believes that God would protect me from all harm. I would say to myself, "Yes, things look bad, but at the last-minute God would break in and rescue me." Looking back, I don't know why I bought into that popular theology but somehow, I expected God to rescue me before I hit the wall. He didn't. But as I've processed the events over time, I see where He did have my best in mind. He did love me. He did have a plan for me, and hitting the wall was a part of achieving that plan.

In This Life Or The Next

Okay. So far, I've said that our own dreams may fail, and that having faith, regardless of the outcome, is better, and that God *is* "a man of His word," (Titus 1:2). But that can still leave us wondering about those God-given promises that probably won't come true in *this* life. Well, thankfully, we're not limited to just *this* life.

What do you do with the feeling that it's over for you, that you'll never have the opportunities again to minister? *My day has come and gone, the music has stopped, and the ride is over.* One of the things that I believe we have not understood very well, and therefore often forget about, is *ETERNITY*. For many believers, including many church leaders, we just don't think about eternity. Yes, we get to go to Heaven when it's over, but that's often the extent of our consideration of the future. And when people do start to consider Heaven, they envision people sitting around on clouds playing harps...forever! I don't know about you, but doing *that* for a billion times a billion years could *really* get on my nerves! (I'm not even sure there will be any harps in eternity. I'm hoping for electric guitars, though.)

This writing isn't the place for us to explore all that the Scriptures teach about eternity, but the Word does say that one day God will create a "new heaven and a new earth," (Rev. 21:1), that He will give us "resurrected/glorified bodies," (1 Cor. 15), and that we will "rule and reign with Him," (Rev. 20:6). Wait a minute, that sounds intriguing, doesn't it? Even now, when we consider this planet, our solar system and the billions upon billions of galaxies that God has created, and somehow you and I will fit into running the thing, well, maybe we won't just be sitting around playing harps.

A Time For Rewards

I believe that the 70+ years that God gives us on this earth are but an internship. It's a place of learning, training and taking tests, some big, some small. Life tests our character, our attitudes, our faithfulness, our obedience, our steadfastness, and our willingness to do things God's way. It also tests us when everything and everyone come against us. The reward of laying down your life for the Kingdom is great. Throughout the Gospels, Jesus gives us parables where men were given gifts and talents to use wisely. For those who did, Jesus said; "Well done good and faithful servant" Matthew 5:21. He then proceeded to increase their talents or invite them to enter the rewards of the Master.

In Col. 3:33-34 it says "Whatever you do, do your work heartily, as unto the Lord, rather than for men, knowing that from the Lord you will receive the reward of the inheritance...." There *are* going to be rewards and there *is* going to be an inheritance. "Behold, I am coming quickly, and My reward is with me, to render to every man according to what he has done," (Rev. 22:12). Our sins and failures have been covered by the finished work of Christ on the cross. What awaits us are the crowns and rewards for that which we've done well.

His callings are "without repentance," (Rom. 11:29), and "His Kingdom (rule and authority) will have no end," (Luke 1:33). Can you choose to trust the very nature and promises of God because He lives outside of time, in eternity? Do you honestly think that a little thing like dying and leaving this body will thwart the plan of God for your life?

Allow yourself to hope that any failed plans in this life will not circumvent the eternal plans that God has for you. You may wonder how the things you felt in your heart could *ever* come to pass. The good news is, you've got eternity to figure it out and discover what the Scriptures repeat over and over: What we see in this life is just a *shadow* of the good things to come. You may want justice now. You may feel that eternity is a long way off. But 70 or 80 years (even if spent in misery) are *nothing* compared to forever and forever and forever again. This is your promise. This present life may not be the place of the fulfillment of your calling and destiny, but there is a day of fulfilled dreams coming. Thank God.

Remember, you were not created just for life here and now. You were created as an eternal being. You were created to rule and reign with Christ. You were created with a destiny, and that destiny still awaits you. We really are like Edmond, Susan, Peter, and Lucy in Narnia. We are going to step through the back of the wardrobe into eternity where our destiny awaits us.

This is the time to put things in perspective. This is the time to forget the things that lie behind and press on to the things that lie ahead. In the bright light of eternity, can you find the grace to forgive those who have hurt you? Are you able to come to peace with the fact that God *will* have His way? Can you trust Him to fulfill all that He has promised to you -- in this life and the next?

Our prayer for you is for complete healing. May the grace of the Lord and the hope of tomorrow comfort you.

APPENDIX

UNGODLY BELIEFS DISCOVERY SHEET:
Lies That I Believe to be True

(Check off each one that seems to apply to your heart)

LIES ABOUT MYSELF:

Theme: Rejection / Not Belonging:

_____ 1. I don't belong. I will always be on the "outside" or left out.

_____ 2. My feelings don't count. No one cares what I feel.

_____ 3. No one will love me or care about me just for myself.

_____ 4. I will always be lonely. The special man (woman) in my life will not be there for me.

_____ 5. I must isolate myself so that I won't be vulnerable to hurt, rejection, etc. anymore.

Theme: Unworthiness, Guilt, Shame:

_____ 1. I am too shameful/guilty to receive anything from God.

_____ 2. I am the problem. When something goes wrong, it's my fault.

_____ 3. I am a bad person. If you knew the real me, you would reject me.

_____ 4. I must wear a mask so that people won't find out how horrible I am and reject me.

_____ 5. I have messed up so badly that I have missed God's purposes for my life.

Theme: DOING to achieve self-worth, value, & recognition:

_____ 1. I will never get credit for what I do.

_____ 2. My value is in what I do. I am valuable because I do good to others, or am successful.

_____ 3. Even when I do or give my best, it is not good enough. I can never meet the standard.

_____ 4. I will choose to be passive to avoid conflict that would risk other's disapproval.

_____ 5. God doesn't care if I have a "secret life", as long as I appear to be good.

Theme: Control (to avoid hurt):

_____ 1. I must plan every day of my life. I must continually plan/strategize. I can't relax.

_____ 2. The perfect life is one in which no conflict is allowed, and so there is peace.

Theme: Physical:

_____ 1. I am unattractive. God shortchanged me.

_____ 2. I will not be accepted until I gain or lose weight.

_____ 3. I cannot be loved with my body the way it is.

Theme: Personality Traits: (fill in the blank)

_____ 1. I will always be _____ (angry, shy, jealous, insecure, fearful, etc.)

Theme: Identity:

_____ 1. I should have been a boy (girl), then my parents would have valued me/loved me more.

_____ 2. Men (women) have it better.

_____ 3. I will never be known or appreciated for my real self.

_____ 4. I will never really change and be as God wants me to be.

Theme: Miscellaneous:

_____ 1. Turmoil is normal for me.

_____ 2. I will always have financial problems.

LIES ABOUT OTHERS:

Theme: Safety / Protection:

_____ 1. I must be very guarded about what I say, since anything I say may be used against me.

_____ 2. I have to guard and hide my emotions and feelings. I cannot give anyone the satisfaction of knowing that they have wounded or hurt me. I'll not be vulnerable, humiliated or shamed.

Theme: Retaliation:

_____ 1. The correct way to respond if someone offends me is to punish them by withdrawing and/or cutting them off.

_____ 2. I will make sure that _____ hurts as much as I hurt.

Theme: Victim:

_____ 1. Authority figures will humiliate me and violate me.

_____ 2. Others will just use and abuse me.

_____ 3. My value is based totally on others' judgment/perception about me.

_____ 4. I am completely under their authority. I have no will or choice of my own.

_____ 5. I will not be known, understood, loved or appreciated for who I am by those close to me.

Theme: Hopelessness / Helplessness:

_____ 1. I am out there all alone. If I get into trouble or need help, there is no one to rescue me.

Theme: Defective in Relationships:

_____ 1. I will never be able to fully give or receive love. I don't know what it is.

_____ 2. If I let anyone get close to me, I may get my heart broken again. I can't let myself risk it.

_____ 3. If I fail to please you, I won't receive your pleasure for and acceptance of me. Therefore, I must strive even more (perfectionism). I must do whatever is necessary to try to please you.

Theme: God:

_____ 1. God loves other people more than He loves me.

_____ 2. God only values me for what I can do. My life is just a means to an end.

_____ 3. No matter how much I try, I'll never be able to do enough or do it well enough to please God.

_____ 4. God is judging me when I relax. I have to stay busy about His work or He will abandon me.

_____ 5. God has let me down before. He may do it again. I can't trust Him, or feel secure with Him.

_____ 6. God doesn't really want to bless me abundantly. He will usually just meet my needs.

_____ 7. God doesn't really want to heal me. He is "teaching me" something deeper by letting me suffer.

_____ 8. I've blown it too many times. I can't be forgiven.

Instructions:

Each one you've checked must be repented of and renounced. Choose to change your mind about these lies.

On a sheet of paper write down each of the lies you've checked off. Leave room to write a response beneath it. Now below write out the corresponding truth of God in that space.

In humility (without argument which is pride) receive each of these new truths into your heart. Pray these new truths each day for 30 days, thanking God for the new truths that you've discovered about yourself. We suggest 30 days so that you have the opportunity to genuinely believe the truth and to make it a part of your life.

www.ingramcontent.com/pod-product-compliance
Lightning Source LLC
Chambersburg PA
CBHW061145040426
42445CB00013B/1565